T.A. FOR TEENS

(AND OTHER IMPORTANT PEOPLE)

Other Works by the Author

Books

TA for Kids (and grown-ups, too)
TA for Tots (and other Prinzes)
TA for Tots Coloring Book

Records and Cassettes

TA for Tots LP Record Album (70 minutes)
TA for Tots Cassette (55 minutes)
TA for Kids Cassette (45 minutes)
All About Feelings Warm Fuzzy Record Album (in production)

Multi Media

TOT-PAC Audio Visual Unit
Parent-PAC Self Concept Unit

TRANSACTIONAL ANALYSIS FOR EVERYBODY SERIES

T.A. FOR TEENS

(AND OTHER IMPORTANT PEOPLE)

BY

ALVYN M. FREED, PH.D.

Illustrations by Regina Faul-Jansen

JALMAR PRESS INC., SACRAMENTO

1st Printing 1976
ISBN 0-915190-03-6
Library of Congress Catalog Card No. 76-19651

Published by Jalmar Press, Inc.
391 Munroe St.
Sacramento, CA 95825

Distribution to Book Trade by
Price/Stern/Sloan Publishers, Inc.
410 N. La Cienaga Blvd.
Los Angeles, CA 90048

Distributed to El/Hi, Churches, Community Service Groups
By Jalmar Press, Inc.

DEDICATION

To you, Mother and Dad, Amy and Jesse Freed, whose Parent Tapes I appreciate more now in the belated realization that without your values and principles, I would have been a ship in a storm without a rudder. I regret so much that you cannot be here to enjoy the success your guidance, love, work, and wisdom made possible.

To my wife, Marge, whose constancy and love through all the years of our marriage contributed so much to my discipline and stability of thought and which have enabled me to write my books and to achieve some degree of fulfillment in living.

To sons, Mark and Larry, to whom I have written my books so that perhaps someday we can achieve the deep, lasting, and profound friendship we all yearn for.

I dedicate my book to you.

Alvyn M. Freed

CREDITS

Life Positions	—	George H. Weldon, George H. Weldon Associates, 1020 - 23rd Street, N.W., Canton, Ohio
Warm Fuzzy Tale	—	Claude M. Steiner, Berkeley, California
Wants List	—	Larry Mart, **Group Treatment and Intimacy**, Sacramento, California, 1974
A Progression of Permissions	—	James R. Allen, M.D. and Barbara Ann Allen, M.S.W., M.P.A., **Scripts, The Role of Permissions**, ITAA Journal, 2:2, April, 1972
EGOGRAM	—	John M. Dusay, M.D. **EGOGRAMS**, Harper and Row, New York, 1977
OK Corral	—	Franklin Ernst, M.D., Vallejo, California
Corralogram	—	Franklin Ernst, M.D., Vallejo, California
Contracts	—	John F. Whittaker, **OK Street Work/Fun Book**
Drama Triangle	—	Stephen B. Karpman, M.D., San Francisco, California
Talk Patterns of People In Crisis	—	William Pemberton, Personnel Administration 1969

ACKNOWLEDGEMENTS

Many people have encouraged me to write *TA for Teens*. Among the most urgent were those people of all ages who have responded so graciously and enthusiastically to our *TA for Kids* and *TA for Tots*. To you, I am truly grateful. Your letters and strokes have made my task a joy. Thank you.

One who has patiently read, commented, argued and fought for changes is my 19-year-old critic and friend, Jan Fling, who out of her wonderfully intuitive Little Professor is able to sense what will and will not go down with people in her age group. Jan, you've been very special and of unlimited help.

Other people who have read and suggested constructive changes and to whom I will be eternally grateful include Sybil Frank, Alice Lancaster, Pam Levin, and Carol Budlong.

For all the patient typing, drafts and re-writes, I thank Peggy Herman, Kris Gifford-Dean, and Barbara J. Lovas — my hardworking secretarial staff.

For a masterful job of designing and book production I acknowledge John Dickinson Adams, General Manager and Editor-In-Chief, Jalmar Press.

I especially wish to thank Marge Freed for her careful and skilled proofing of the galleys.

To Regina Faul-Jansen, unstinting praise for her beautiful, creative, and exciting illustrations which make the book a work of art as well as a helpful tool.

I am grateful to all my colleagues in the International Transactional Analysis Association for their continuing pioneer work to develop new concepts and techniques which are reflected in my book.

Finally, I render a salute to Dr. Eric Berne who started the whole thing.

AMF

TABLE OF CONTENTS

TABLE OF CONTENTS

LIST OF FIGURES/DIAGRAMS

Foreword
By T. R. Shantha, M.D., Ph.D.

This work, like the best possible parent, reveals an accurate understanding of the many aspects of teenage life: dilemma, drama, fantasy, reality, excitement, sex and much more. I cannot think of a single aspect of a problem that happens to most teenagers, as well as to adults, that is not well covered here. This is excellent reading material for parents, many of whom are unaware of modern day teenage situations which produce stress and conflict. *TA for Teens* is a guide for all in best coping with teen years and in handling serious teen problems.

As Dr. Freed demonstrates, many current teenage problems are brought about by lack of intimate contact between parents and teenagers often because both mother and father are working and are frequently away from the home. When they return, they find little time to spend with their teenagers. Many problems brought to parents by teenagers in the evening are handled improperly; often they are merely pushed aside as nothing significant, or over magnified.

Grandparents who used to stay with their children and grandchildren as part of the family, are now more and more living in nursing homes and homes for the elderly. These grandparents formerly played an important role in modulating the psyche of the teenager during the early part of this century. The almost nonexistent problems in Asian families is attributed largely to the existence of grandparents in the home. They play an important role in giving STROKES as described in this book. "Strokes," which is also called "touching experience," is very important for all phases of normal human behavior development.

All chapters are thorough and amply illustrated. Chapters 1, 6, 12, 16 and 18 are truly outstanding — probably the best work available on these subjects. Exercises at the end of each chapter help to reinforce attitudes of objective thinking and lead to workable solutions even for many unusual situations.

Teens are generally "O.K.," "normal," and "all right." Teen years are trying and difficult. This work can bring teens, parents, relatives, teachers, community religious leaders and friends into closer and more satisfying relationships.

Dr. Freed introduces basic theories of TA and uses the concepts to expand on such topics as sex, hassletimes, drugs, relationships with adults and peers, talking straight, decisions and contracts, getting strokes, games, leadership, death, desertion and divorce.

Transactional Analysis should be part of the curriculum for all high school and college students. I highly recommend this book as essential for all families with teenagers and for high school, college and public libraries. Youth counselors and medical libraries will consider this work to be a classic treatment of this subject.

T. R. Shantha, M.D., Ph.D., F.A.C.A., D.A.B.A. (USA), F.Z.S. (London), F.R.M.S. (England)

Associate Professor, Emory University School of Medicine
Staff Member, Georgia Baptist Hospital
Staff Member, Columbus Medical Center
Author, YOUR BREAST AND ITS CARE
Founder, The National Breast Care Foundation
Associate Editor-in-Chief, Cato's Communications Encyclopedia

INTRODUCTION

TA for Teens (and Other Important People) is the fifth book in the TA for Everybody series. In *TA for Tots (and Other Prinzes)*, and *TA for Kids (and Grownups, Too)*, I reintroduced in a simplistic way the basic concepts of Transactional Analysis primarily to young people in the pre-school through late elementary years. Many people, regardless of age or academic sophistication, have found the texts useful in understanding themselves and the people around them.

My original intent was to provide tools to be used in school and at home by young people in learning to cope with dilemmas which plague them in childhood. I am told that they are equally useful for resolving the difficulties encountered by those of advancing years.

In the current book, I continue to direct the reader's attention to the powerful tools of TA. I hope they will be used in the resolution of your daily dilemmas of living in school, at home, at work, and at play.

The dilemmas of the young are horrific. No less so are those of the People in Charge of them. We must not and do not underestimate the difficulties both youth and age are encountering in the process of functioning in a mixed-up world. Mothers and fathers, principals and teachers, law makers and administrators are people, too, with hopes and dreams, feelings and frustrations, responsibilities and rights, weaknesses and strengths, foolishness and wisdom. We who lead are equally puzzled and at times overwhelmed by a world which seemingly contracts as it expands, where old rules don't fit and new ones are frightening, albeit seemingly ideally correct.

Our situation, it seems, is similar to that of Ulysses and his men who were being lured to the shallow rocks by the beautiful Circe. We seem to be flirting with the beauties of freedom and irresponsibility while knowing we need the skill, determination, and inner strength to follow more conventional sea lanes through deeper, calmer, safer (duller) waters to reach a home port of tranquility and fulfillment.

With each recent generation of students, we have seen their successive waves of righteous rebellion break against a rocklike status quo which masked what appeared to be and later actually was disclosed to be hypocrisy and corruption, as well as blind adherence to outmoded loyalties and destructive institutional policies.

On the other hand, we see the results of the breakdown in control at home and school reflected in the increase in crime, drugs, aggressive sex (rape, prostitution, slavery, perversion), and emotional disturbance.

Thus, it appears to me that unless we provide ourselves with common, easily acquired tools and skills of understanding and thought that the product of our 200 years of progress may well be lost. TA is such a tool - simple, colloquial as American apple pie, fun, exciting, and practical. With TA, I think we can recapture the spirit of America.

There is nothing wrong with our American values and our American system. We have to understand ourselves and each other and continue to care enough about each other to make the system work, not because we're afraid not to, but because we do **care** about ourselves and all other people.

Alvyn M. Freed

If our lives have become shallow,
Deepen them.

If our principles have become shabby,
Repair them.

If our ideals have become tarnished,
Restore them.

If our hopes have become faded,
Revive them.

If our loyalties have grown dim,
Brighten them.

If our values have become confused,
Clarify them.

If our purposes have become blurred,
Sharpen them.

If our horizons have become contracted,
Widen them.

If our hearts have become chilled by
Indifference, fear, and disappointment,
Warm them with mercy and faith and love
For ourselves and for each other.

Unknown

Chapter I

WINNERS, LOSERS AND OTHER PEOPLE

"Begin: to begin is half the work."   Ausonius

OF PRINZES AND FROZZES

You were born a Prinz* (a winner). Yet you may *feel* like a froz (a loser). At times, you may tell yourself, "I'm no good. I can't win. I never do anything right. Nothing good will ever happen to me, and there's nothing I can do about it." But you can change your belief and win. You can change from a Froz to a Prinz.

"You can change your belief and be a winner!"

* Peoples' Lib for Prince or Princess.

We are nothing but a point of view. We are what we think we are. Change your thinking about yourself and you'll change how you are. "But it's so hard," you say. "I have so much proof I'm no good." Well, each event is separate from the last one. So, start over right now. And you are not a loser. You are not a winner. You may not always win, but neither will you always lose. "Oh yeah?" you may say. "Show me!"

From the day you were born, you've always been OK. Many people lose that feeling of being OK because of some of the things that happen to them in the process of growing up. Somehow or other, perhaps because of what happened since the moment you first leaped into life, you may have decided that you're really not worth much; that you're a loser; "I'll never be happy;" "Nothing good will ever happen to me;" "I'm no good, a failure." You may say these things to yourself, over and over, because of many feelings of unhappiness early in your life. In the words of Transactional Analysis (TA), you may have decided that you are a Froz*. You often go around with a lot of frozzy (downer) feelings. Frozzes don't ever get what they want, and losers don't ever get what they want, either. They often lose and help others to lose, too.

Losers usually think they are the only ones who feel that way. Lots of people who feel that they are "born losers" think that they can never be a success. They think, "I can never be as good as anybody else, I'll never be as successful as my father or as clever as mother or as strong or as smart as my older brother."

Once I was asked to do a psychological study of a man who had committed six murders, several of them while in prison. He was well known to everyone as a skilled killer — a top "hit man." By most usual standards, he was a loser in society and life. As I was leaving, he mentioned, "My brother is a rich rancher out in the West here. He's really well off." Then he added something I'll always remember. "I'll never be the man he is, though." In the few minutes we had left together, before he went back to his cell, he told me that he had been trying to compete with his brother all his life. He couldn't win by being good, so he was going to be the best bad guy in the West. The sad part of this is that he could have been a winner, but decided, when he was very young, to win by losing *because he could never prove to himself that he was not a loser.* All through his life he kept listening to a message in his head saying: "You're no good. You're not as good as your brother. You'll never be as good as he is." In one sense he was a winner. He was at the top of his chosen line of work and received the State's highest award — Guilty of Murder, Life Imprisonment. Since pro hit men reputedly don't get caught, and since he was caught each time, I suspect him of playing a hard (3rd degree) game of "Cops and Robbers." He could still get well by a changed point of view. But of course, it wouldn't be easy.

What about you? Do your early decisions keep you from being a winner? Do you tell yourself, "No matter what I do, I'll never be happy. I'll never be a success. I'll never be satisfied or contented. I'm just a Froz, and I'm no

*Peoples' Lib for a male or female Frog

2

"He decided when he was very young to win by losing."

good." If so, you can change your point of view (see things differently — ask for other opinions) and you may start winning.

You may wonder, "Why do I keep those Frozzy feelings? How did I get them?" I wonder, if you have them, how long you will keep them? Do you know you can give them up? When will you give them up? If you set a date *right now* for giving them up, you're well on your way to becoming a winner.

I am writing this book to help you to change, if you want to. *You can change,* if you *know how* and if you *"do it."* I'll try to help you learn how. You can if you will. It takes courage (guts) and determination (hanging in there). Anybody can give up. But winners get what they want without keeping other people from winning. In fact, winners help others win, too. So, go with winners and go to win. One way to get winners is by finding out how to be a winner. Be aware that you may have decided to become a loser sometime ago, like at the age of 3. If so, it's time to *change your point of view.* You decided to lose way back. Now, I can show you how to change; to get into the winner's circle.

BECOMING A WINNER

If you want to win, *decide right now to give up putting yourself down.* Throw out of your word-list the phrases, "I can't" or "I'll try." Doers *"do."* Tryers lose. Put in "I will" and "I'll do it!" Choose to "win."

"I never finish anything I start," said a man the other day, "so I'm a loser." I pointed out that starting is a skill and an asset. Lots of people are great organizers, others are sustainers. Sustainers are "keep it going types" who have little start up ability and don't know how to get things going. For instance, I knew a man who loved to start a business and then sell it after he had built it. Then he'd move and start another one. The people who bought it were sustainers. They would run it following the set of rules developed by the original owner. There is a place for both. There's even a place for finishers — ever see a skilled wrecking crew take a building apart? So, if you always wreck everything, well maybe . . . Did you know that in the book publishing and selling business, some people sell new books and some "remainders" (that is, books that won't sell easily)? Then there are some people who shred up books which won't sell at all and sell the pulp. (Hope that doesn't happen to TA for Teens tho!) See? Everybody can win, but not necessarily in the same way nor even in the same ball game.

First of all, let's look at where you are now as a person. Then, if you want to change, we can look at some new thinking tools. I'll tell you about them as we go along.

THREE PEOPLE INSIDE OF US

You can understand how you got to be where you are if you look at yourself as one person with three separate people inside you. Each of these three people is you — at different times. For example, if you've just smashed up your fender by backing into a tree and you're raging mad, you're coming on from your Child or the Kid. If you then feel like you should let somebody know about the damages to the tree, you're coming on from your Parent. Then, if you decide to fix the fender and wonder what it will cost — you're in your Adult. These three people run or ruin your life because they decide things for you, think for you, feel for you, and act for you. There are not three actual little people running around inside you, but three completely different ways of thinking, feeling, and believing. And, each of these different ways feel like you! They can cause you to act differently at different times. It's like there are three different selves (elves?) inside you. And to know which of the three is feeling (C), thinking (A) or guiding (P) right now, is a good place to begin knowing how "yourself" works. Next time you say "I", wonder which one is speaking.

Dr. Eric Berne[2] is the person who first described the three people inside of us. He named them Parent, Adult, and Child. He said they were Ego (Self) States. Notice, each of the three Ego States I spelled with a capital letter. The phrase Child Ego State doesn't mean youngster, baby, or toddler as it usually does, and Adult doesn't mean an "older person". Parent doesn't mean father or mother. These words with their capital letters P,A, and C stand for the names of the three different "people" inside of you. They tell you what to do and help you to do it. They are our decision makers. Each one is a sort of Captain of a team, who is in charge at the time. The Captain calls the plays and leads the action. Who's in charge in you determines whether you win or not. If your Child is leading your parade when the action calls for quick thinking, you're not likely to win. In fact, if you let the three-year-old Kid inside you do your deciding for you, you may get in trouble.

Suppose you think of something you are doing and want to know "why,"

"Inside you there are three separate people."

you can speak to yourself like this: "I want to go to a movie." Now, to know which self is speaking, you'll need some clues. Clues are the words we use, like "I want (C), I should (P), I think(A)." You may, at another time, say to your younger brother, "Get out of my room and don't come in here again (P).".Or, perhaps another time, you might say to your Dad, "Dad, what do you think about what's happening in Washington right now (A)?" In each case, one of your selves, called Ego States (ego means self), is talking. I have put a list of clues and cues on the next page which will help you to find out which one of your Ego States is talking, deciding, or behaving for you. If you look at the list and learn them, you'll be taking another first step in finding out about you and who is running your life. Finding out about you will help you to feel better about yourself and to learn about other people. That sounds pretty worthwhile to me. Does it to you? Why?

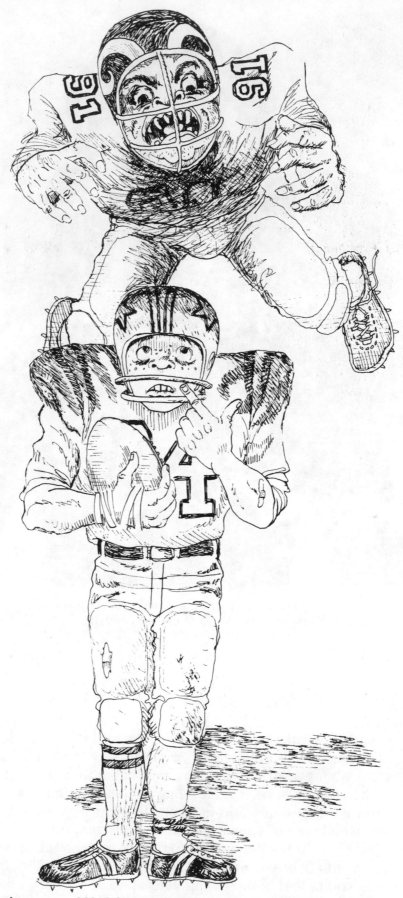

"If you let a three year old kid do your deciding, you may get into trouble."

"Clues are words we use."

TABLE 1
CUES AND CLUES TO EGO STATES

Our actions are directed by the person (Ego State) "in charge" at the time. Most of us have difficulty distinguishing between our Parent (P), Adult (A), and Child (C). To find out "who's talking," listen to your own words and those of others. Here are some words and behaviors which will help you to tell one Ego State from another:

PARENTAL VERBALIZATIONS: Parental actions, beliefs, values, dogma, prejudices, are learned from Mother and Father or other "People In Charge." Check out the words and phrases you use to see if you're "coming on Parent."

annoying	low	be good
childish	shocking	always
unreasonable	disgusting	let me help you
how dare you!	disobedient	come on now
No! No!	brat	sweetheart
vulgar	do this!	sonny
ridiculous	dearie	poor thing

7

thief	never	selfish
if I were you	don't ask questions	WHY
eat! it's good for you!	see, it doesn't hurt	shouldn't one
shut up!	honey	proverbs
naughty	"little darling"	there, there
lazy	indulgent laughing	don't
pouting	derisive laughing	must
noisy	don't be afraid	now what
sulking	what will the neighbors say?	do not disturb
nonsense	bad	don't worry
stupid	good	my baby
shameful	troublemaker	cute
careless	stubborn	poor old
thoughtless	filthy	not again!
uncooperative	*ought*	I'll take care of you
because I said so!	*should (n't)*	why? (in criticism)
sweetie	duty	here's something to
try		make you feel better.

CHILD VERBALIZATIONS AND BEHAVIORS: Words and actions from your Child usually are labels for your feelings. They are often intended to obtain satisfaction from pleasant feelings or relief from unpleasant feelings such as tension, fear, loneliness, anger, frustration, or to express these feelings. How many "Child" words do you use? Check it out against the following list:

gosh	right on!	he's no good
I don't care	I'm going to tell on you	I want to go home
I can't	why? (in protest)	I promise_____if you
I want	won't	I hope everybody loves me
I don't want	everybody	dunno
I don't know	nobody does	gimme
I wish	temper tantrums	coyness
I hope	swearing	self pity
I'm gonna	begging	self praise
I guess	pouting	bragging
I hate	weeping	imagination
Yum! Yum!	sulking	sex
Ouch!	whining	sensual pleasure
they	creativity pleasure	joy
happy laugh	*I'll try*	baby talk
day dreams	all the time	happiness
fear	irreverent laughing	love
bigger	games	teasing
best	fantasy	giddy laughing
wow	when I grow up	nervous (I'm)
eek	hurt	sad
ain't I cute?	quarreling	depressed
do it for me	biggest	anger
it's your fault	overeating	better
I didn't do it	gee whiz	mine
more candy	did I do all right?	look at me now!
mine is better than yours	I'm scared	help me
you'll be sorry	nobody loves me	you make me cry

8

let's play
phooey on this old job
far out!

neat!
cool!
·man!
tough!

ADULT VERBALIZATIONS: The Adult attempts to deal with the present. It "calls 'em the way it sees 'em" without trying to change the truth. It is honest, accurate, "makes sense." The Adult doesn't place values on behavior. It describes things as they are. Listen with your Adult to find out "who's talking." Here are some Adult words and phrases:

childlike
easier
helpful
productive
objective
correct
destructive
authentic
honest
I choose
laugh of discovery
how much
I see
alternative
what are the facts?
this is not proven
have you tried this?
what has been done
  to correct it so far?
according to the
  statistics . . .

rational
realistic
real
responsible
factual
true
better
my choice is
I'd rather
false
error
I think
result
yes
check it out
what are the reasons?
mix two parts with
  one part
let's take it
  apart and
  look at it

improving
what
how
who
which
where
when
could be more
why (for information)
unknown
possible
comparative
probability
no
it's 4:30 p.m.
this is how it works
let's look for the causes
change is indicated

When you were first born, you were a Prinz (*) — you were OK. OK means worthwhile, able to think, and important to yourself and others. You were OK with yourself and with everyone else. You had great worth just because you were. Of course, come children are not planned. Unmarried mothers feel lots of social or financial distress when they have a baby. *But the baby is OK.* It didn't make the rules and couldn't care less about them. People make the distress — people and rules which label an OK baby a "bastard." Some folks want boys and get girls. Some want girls and get twin boys. Some babies are crippled or diseased. Some are slow learning. *But all babies are OK.* What happens to you from then on changes your feelings about yourself.

When you were first born, you were able to feel. You could feel everything better than you can now. You enjoyed the feelings of warmth, taste, food, the soothing, nice feeling of being bathed, or of being played with by mother, dad, older brother or sister. You probably loved having your back rubbed. Maybe you still do. Later, you enjoyed milk or peanut

(*Prinz) — Peoples' Lib for Prince and Princess. Eric Berne said we are all born Princesses and Princes. I prefer to say Prinz.

butter and jelly sandwiches on whole wheat bread. Unfortunately for me and my diet, I was raised on starchy carbohydrates like candy, cake, and white bread. I still like these things too much. I had awful teeth (no fluoride then). Like me, you may have lost something you treasured like a puppy or a friend and felt terribly sad. You probably felt hurt over things you couldn't have or wanted to do. You may also have felt pain much more intensely than now. Remember when you fell down and banged your knee when you were three? Ooh! That used to sting! Now, when you bang your knee, it may sting or smart, and you say "Ow," but while that "Ow" is much like what you said when you were a little kid, you don't feel the same intensity of pain.

TA STROKES KEEP US ALIVE

In TA, the word "stroke" means what someone else does that causes you to feel. It may be someone's hand rubbing your back, a kick in the shins (Ouch!), a smile or a kind word, but each one causes you to feel.

When you were a baby, you needed strokes to keep you alive. Without them, you would have developed a disease known as marasmus (shrinking of your spinal cord). You need strokes to live. When you are little you have no way of getting what you need for yourself. You surely can't run out to the nearest grocery store to get something to eat, or even walk to the sink for a glass of water. And you surely can't scratch your own back. Now that you're almost full grown, you still must have strokes to stay healthy. So, you still need to get strokes from other people if you're going to live. That's why Mom and Pop and friends mean so much to you*.

Strokes come in a variety of kinds. Pleasant, unpleasant, free, and earned. They are so important to us that we spend 24 hours a day figuring out ways of getting them. Later on we'll talk more about them.

The Child in us is the little Prinz between years 0 to 5 who learned feelings. Early feelings are important. They stay with us all of our lives. Did you ever say, "I've *always* been afraid of mice, cats, bugs, the dark?" It's not true. You may have had one unpleasant experience and from then on decided you did not like mice, or cats, or so on. Later, you may learn through your Adult that *some* kittens are nice and warm and snuggly, but you'll also have Child memory-feelings of being scratched. So, your Child can go on recording new and pleasant or unpleasant feelings all your life, but the early ones play a very important part in your life and your later feelings about things.

The Parent: Now who are the people, mainly, who gave us strokes? Right again! Mother, Dad, brothers, sisters, Aunt or Uncle, Grandma and Grandpa, and so on. But in our early life it's mainly Mom and Dad. If you are one of the luckier ones, it will be all of them. Because some husbands and wives get divorced or die soon after babies are born, you may not have lived with your Mother or your Dad when you were young. But *somebody*

---

*Pam Levin and Robert Landheer are writing a book on strokes. They're warm fuzzy people. You should read their book when it comes out because strokes are so important.

"Who are the people who gave us strokes? Mother, Dad, brothers, sisters, Aunt or Uncle, Grandma and Grandpa, and so on."

gave you strokes or you wouldn't be here to read this book right now! You can think and talk about who gave you strokes and what you had to do to get them. For now, let's think it was Mother and Dad who were the PIC (People-In Charge) of you when you were 0 to 5 years old.

When you are a baby, you feel that your Mom and Dad are the only Somebodys in the world. When those special Somebodys keep you alive by supplying you with what you need (air, water, food, strokes), they become very important to you. What these people-in-charge (PIC) show you, how they act, and what they believe, can become for you the only way to do, speak, feel, think, or believe. You see, hear, and feel the way they speak, hold, or touch you. They are soft or hard, calm or nervous; clean or dirty. They smell sweet or bad. They hit or hug; smile or frown; move slowly or rapidly; breathe heavy or light. And they become a part of you. In other words, you begin to form the part in you we called the Parent (P). Your Parent (P) is the part that tells you how to do things and how to behave even when Mother and Dad are not around. It can tell you what they would do if they were doing it, or what they would want you to do. The Parent tells you the "right" way to cross the street, use a telephone, or bake a chocolate cake like Cousin Marcy's. We know how *they think we should* behave. What is in our Parent is what we learned from Mother and Father (and other important people) about how to behave the way they *want us to behave,* or how *they would behave* if they were doing it. Those learnings become part of the "person in you" called your Parent. For the rest of your life, you may or may not believe that what they do or did is the "right" way. And it may be you are right, but you now know where it came from. If you believe, for example, in "justice for all" you learned that phrase and its meaning from grownups. That phrase is "on tape" in your Parent. In TA we call them "Parent Tapes" which you use as guides. What did Mom and Dad always say that you'll "never forget?" Make a list to see if you agree with them now.

"What is in our Parent is what we learned from Mother and Father."

"I'LL NEVER BE LIKE THAT"

You may not have liked what those important people did, or thought, but you learned what those things were because it was so important to you at the time. You may have taken in some notions as facts which are open to question. Maybe most of what they told you helps you. Some you may not understand. What are some things your mother always told you about you? Mark Twerk's father told him, "Remember, you are a Twerk! You are better than those trashy kids on the next block." Jeli Bunn's mama told her, "Be sweet." Jirk* Soda's pop pounded into him, "Always respect your elders." What did you take into your Parent? What are some of your Parent Tapes? On Page   is a list of words that people say who are thinking in their Parent, their Adult, and their Child. How many do you use? Finding out is another step in learning who is running your life — for they are part of "Who You Are."

THE PARENT IS BOTH CRITICAL AND NURTURING

Many things your father, mother, grandmother, grandfather, uncle, aunt, brother, sister, or teacher told you from their Parent may be helpful to you. They may help you to make honest choices. Their ideas are probably helping to keep you alive, safe, and secure. Many times these thoughts can comfort you when you are alone. "My Mom loves me," or "My Dad thinks I'm OK," or "I can depend on my Dad," and so on. Or, as a guide, "Gee, I don't know how to do it (C). What would Dad do? Well, he'd . . . "
Get the Idea? We take lots of Parental guides into our heads to protect us, to keep us warm and safe, even when PICs are not around and without even knowing where these ideas come from. That's why we love our PICs, because we know they care about us; because they keep us alive and feeling safe, and just because we're theirs. We like knowing they won't desert us when we need them: that they'll always protect us, help us, encourage us, praise us, and so on. Because they do this, we learn, finally, how to care for ourselves with our own Parent. If we know TA, we can learn to use its teachings to protect ourselves. You healthy people are the ones whose Parent tells your Child you're OK. You're a winner. You're safe, good, worthwhile. In other words, the nurturing (pronounced NUR-CHER-ing) Parent in us guides us, gives us feelings of confidence in ourselves, and most of all never deserts us in time of trouble. The Parent in us *loves us* and *loves other people*. The Parent protects us. The Parent helps us and others. So, you see, the Parent is a very fine part of us. And it's OK to love yourself. You won't love anyone else till you love yourself and are convinced you're OK!

There are really two jobs the Parent does. One supports us, the other guides us. The part of the Parent I've just described is the Nurturing, supporting, caring Parent. The other Parent is often called the Critical

*A "Jirk," according to E. Berne, is someone who goes through life attempting to please and appease "Parent type" people.

I AM HAPPY · MY PARENTS LOVE ME · I HA

NURTURING PAREN

Parent (CP). That's the one which tells us when we're doing it right or wrong. The Critical Parent tells us we're bad, nasty, not OK, and so on, if we don't do it "right." Do you give yourself and others too hard a time? You can change if you want to. Get your CP off your back and off theirs!

THE ADULT FIGURES THINGS OUT

Then there's the part of us which grows into what we call the Adult (A).
The Adult in us is that person (self, me, I) who is in touch with "where it's at" right now. People with healthy, strong Adults have gotten their stuff* together. They *can* think (and do). They don't let their Kid make nutty decisions. They avoid getting hurt or getting themselves or someone else busted or pregnant. The Adult in us "figures things out" ahead of time. When your Adult gets the facts (including "How I feel") from your Kid and the "rules" which apply from your Parent, your Adult self can make wise decisions.

When you are in school, your Adult listens and learns from the instructor, from books, or other factual sources. You "pay attention" with your Adult. When you respond to a question either verbally or in writing with accurate facts, your Adult is working. Now, when you start worrying about whether you "got it right" or if you'll get an "A" or an "F", which self is in charge? You're probably thinking (A) "Why that's my Kid (C)", and you're right. I think you can also see that if you put your energy into your Kid by worrying, you don't have much left to do powerful thinking. Fear, worry, anger, hurt, excitement, tension, resentment are all in the Child. The Child gets "jealous" (angry and afraid); the Child is envious (*wants* what other have); the Child seeks strokes, shows off, argues, gets

14

"The Parent protects us."

discouraged, gives up, quits, gets back at, cheats, and so on.

If you're day dreaming *right now* as you read this line — where were you? (To answer, you have to go into your Adult, hence the past tense.) In your Child! Right!

"I CAN'T SAY "NO!"

Some people are very agreeable. They always say yes to PICs because they figure they'll get rewarded for being good. This is called being in the Adapted Child (Passive). In other words, one adapts to the Parent in one's self or someone else. Sometimes people get disappointed at the return on their investment of being "good" and make another "Child" decision. This is called the Rebellious Adapted Child. This person usually does the opposite to what he is asked. I've often heard teachers and mothers say, "I don't know what's gotten into him (her). He (she) used to be so good. And now I can't do a thing with her (him)." Just a shift from AC (Passive) to AC (Rebellious).

Talk about that for a little while. Find out where you are right now about grades, school, mother, father, sisters, brothers. (What are you feeling??? Angry? Hurt? Complaining? Proud? Comfortable?) How are you coming on? I mean, which of your three people is in charge right now? Your Parent, Adult, or Child? Adapted Child? Passive or Rebel?

IF YOU'RE BORED, YOUR KID NEEDS STROKES

When you were little, if something hurt you, you probably cried. If something felt good, you smiled or even laughed. You still do some of those things. These feelings, all of them (hurt, anger, fear, sex, love, excitement,

*Cleaned up word for all Parental readers and Boards of Education.

hate, imagination, want, like, dislike) are the you we call the Child. Sometimes, in slang, we call it "the Kid." The way to tell if your Kid is in charge right now is to focus on how you feel right now. What are you feeling? Excited, curious, interested or bored by this book? If you're bored, it's because your Kid isn't having any fun — you're not getting any good feelings out of reading this page. Do you know what to do about this? Maybe you can figure out why you're bored by talking about your feelings to somebody else.If you're excited or pleased, that's a feeling. You may say, "I like this." That's probably your Free Child.

The Free Child (FC) in all of us is the funloving part of our Kid. It is usually very apparent in small children because it is also the part of the kid which can be very impulsive even willful. The Free Child (FC) may be angry, very loving, playful, hurt, or afraid.

Now, when you were age 1 or 2, you were almost helpless. You had no way to stay alive unless someone helped you. What you needed to keep you going were the main things, food, water, air warmth, and stimulation (strokes). Now, I'm sure you knew about the first four, but maybe not about stimulation. Stimulation, or stroking, is something which someone does to you which causes you to feel. There are physical (touch) strokes and psychological strokes (praise, smiles, a bawling out, and so on).

Now you know something about where you are and how you got here. The rest of this book is how to make use of this information; to feel more OK wherever you happen to be. Whether it is at school, at home, on the job, on a date, in a fight, making a speech, driving a car, or in trouble, you can be a winner every time! You can take some of these tools if you want to change and learn them and make use of them. The rest of our book is intended to tell you how.

EGOGRAM OR SELF CHART

Here is a handy tool for finding out who you are. Do this a number of times every day. Stop and think about what you're feeling (hurt, angry, mad, sad, excited, bossy, sexy, hungry, loving, helpful, concerned, worried, nervous, up-tight, or bored). Where are you coming on from — NP, CP, A, AC, FC. Maybe you can make a chart (see illustration below) of how you operate most of the time. Dr. Jack Dusay calls it the Egogram. You can call it your Self Chart. Carol Budlong suggests we call it the Horror Scope. Maybe you'll want to change your Self Chart and be happier. As you read on, we hope you'll find out how.

16

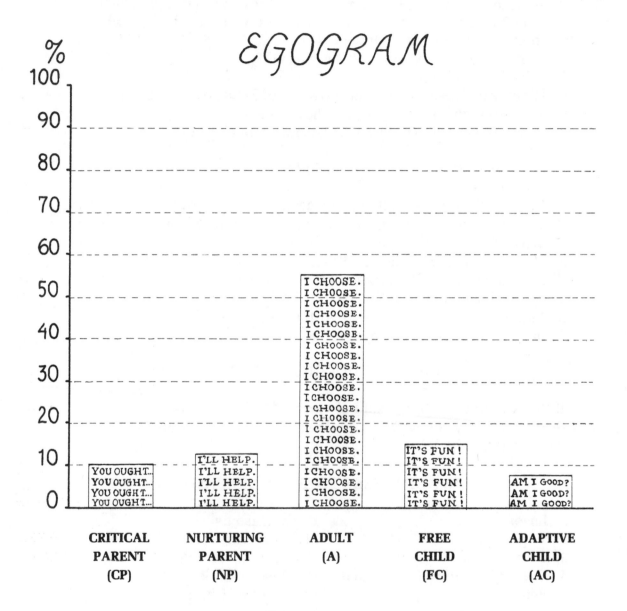

EGOGRAM

"You can call it your Self Chart"

QUESTIONS FOR YOUR ADULT

1. How do you view yourself, Loser, Winner?
2. If a Loser, can you change? How?
3. What causes you to have Frozzy feelings? How do you get rid of them? There are other ways. Discover these by talking about them with other important people.
4. What does OK mean to you? Are you OK?
5. What's a Jirk?
6. What is a stroke? What kinds are there? How do you get yours? If not enough how can you get what you want?
7. How can you tell where you are coming from? (P-A-C)

EXERCISES

1. Make your own self chart (Egogram) now before you read the rest of the book. Then make one at the end and see if it and you are different.
2. List your favorite Child and Parent words and phrases for example: Child - Ouch! Wow!; Parent - Poor dear, ridiculous, disgusting. Where did you learn them?
3. Make a list of Parent tapes (platitudes, common sayings that you have learned, like "always respect your elders").

PROBLEMS FOR THOUGHT AND DISCUSSION

If "we are nothing but a point of view", does this mean I can change the way I am by changing my thinking? Will I feel different? How can I do this?

IDEAS AND WORDS TO LEARN MORE ABOUT

1. Loser
2. Winner
3. Froz
4. Parent (P), Adult (A), Child (C)
5. Ego States
6. Clues and Cues
7. OK, Okay
8. Prinz, Princess, Prince
9. Strokes
10. Marasmus
11. Nurturing, Critical Parent
12. Egogram or Self Chart
13. Passive Child
14. Adapted Child
15. Rebel Child
16. Jirk
17. P-I-C (People or Person in Charge)
18. Transactional Analysis (TA)

Chapter II

WHAT IS TRANSACTIONAL ANALYSIS?

*"Today is the tomorrow I worried about yesterday
that never came."   Amy Freed*

WHAT IS TRANSACTIONAL ANALYSIS? *

In its simplest terms, Transactional Analysis (TA) is a way to know and understand how and why you think and act the way you do; and to understand how and why other people do what they do. TA is useful for everyone, but especially for people who are puzzled about themselves and their relationships with others.

EXCHANGE OF STROKES IS A TRANSACTION

When one person speaks to another, a number of things happen to both people. TA leads to your understanding what goes on inside you. When this happens, the talk that goes on between you and somebody else becomes easy to understand. This line with an arrowhead → is a sign that Person A has said something to Person B like, "How are you?" Person B hears this and says, "Fine, thank you. How are you?" The two sentences look like this:

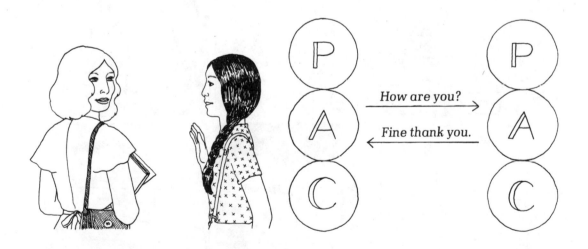

*TRANSACTIONAL ANALYSIS (TA) is the title coined by the late Eric Berne, a psychiatrist. Dr. Berne sensed what all children know: that having fun is essential for mental health. He encourages his patients and colleagues to "let your Kid out."

These arrows are an important tool of TA. We call them "strokes". We call this exchange of ideas, or strokes, a Transaction (i.e., action across). A Transaction is the basic unit of all interpersonal "talk." We are now the sum of all the transactions we've had since we were born. Understanding our transactions helps us know about ourselves and how to get along with others. We are the result of all the transactions we've had since our Day One. Analysis means taking the transaction apart to understand it. A Transaction is an exchange (words, gestures, nods, smiles, frowns, winks, touch, salutes, body movement, etc.) between people. We use the word Transaction because any time people contact each other, they are doing some business; they are being busy with each other, So, a transaction is made up of at least two strokes. One, *I "talk"* to or touch you,* and the other, *you "talk" to or touch me.* Thus, we exchange pieces of information, or feelings, perhaps.

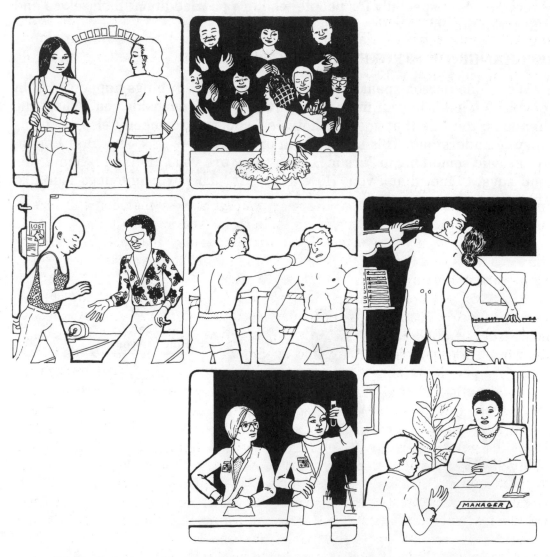

"A stroke is something that makes you know that the other person is there."

*"Talk" here means getting or sending a message.

USING "YOU" AND "I" TALK

A Transaction is an exchange of *"strokes"* which cause people to feel. A stimulus stroke and a response stroke make a Transaction. A *stroke* makes you know that the other person is there. It can be a physical touch or merely a smile. It can be a word of praise or a shout. But, somehow or other, when someone causes you to be aware that he is here, you have received a stroke. When you cause somebody else to know that you are there, you have given her a stroke. This is a very simple way of talking about talking. And that is what TA is all about; to help us understand ourselves and each other. One thing you may have noticed, I keep using 1st person and 2nd person pronouns (I and You). I suggest you do that, too. You will find you make more sense to yourself and others, and you will begin to get in touch with and be responsible for your own feelings. Avoid using "it" when you mean "I", like, "It makes me mad when . . . " Try, "I get mad when . . . " In that way, you'll be in charge of your feelings and then you can change them. Your getting along with others depends on your understanding yourself. And so, when I have talked about winners and losers and the three personalities with you, I have been talking about a way to understand yourself.

SOME TA IDEAS

When we are born, we are OK. Dr. Tom Harris, who wrote the bestselling book, *I'm OK - You're OK*, tells us what OK means. He says that OK means (1) that you are *adequate.* in other words, you are good enough to do the job, to think; (2) you are *worthwhile;* you have worth to yourself and to other people; and (3) you are *important* merely because you are a human being. Simply because you exist. Because you have value to yourself and others, *you are important.* You are important because you cause others to think and feel and thus to become human. In the same way, other people are important to you. We are *all born OK.* As we said in Chapter I, we are relatively helpless when we are infants, so we can't get the things we need (water, food, strokes) for ourselves in order to live. The persons most likely to provide us with these goodies are Mother and Father, and other important people (OIP) around us. So, we begin to try to please these important people. When we succeed in pleasing them, we assure ourselves of a steady flow of positive strokes or "warm fuzzies." We feel that then we are OK. But, as soon as we begin to think that we are *OK only if we please* other people, we change our original idea from "I'm OK" to "I'm OK if . . . (If I get an A, make a touchdown, win at tennis, etc.)" And, that's when we begin to get in trouble. Many of us then get the feeling that we are "Not OK unless." Then, since we aren't able to please grownups (and feel we never will), because when we're in our Child we deal only in absolutes (never, always) we are convinced that we are really "Not OK." *That's our decision.* We are *not born* "Not OK". We decide we're "Not OK" after we're born, and that's the big secret because if I *decided* I'm *Not OK,* I can change my mind *now!* But after that 2-year-old decision of "Not OK", we begin to hide behind our faces and act as if we were OK, while we *feel* inside of us that we are not. It's no big secret that most people go around feeling just that way. Most people believe they are OK "if and only if." They they may believe they will really never be OK. We can never be as good as we should be in some aspect of our behavior (according to somebody else's idea of what "*good*" is). We then tell ourselves we are "*no good*". Most people *think they are the only ones who feel this way*, i.e., that everybody else is OK. Not true.

THE THREE PEOPLE IN US

To understand yourself, you must learn a basic TA idea. As we said earlier, within each of us there are three different people — not real people, but three different personalities (ego states). To know who you are right now, you must understand that these different people tell us how to behave. They are like three separate persons. Each one has his or her own habits, attitudes and usual ways of acting.

PARENT, ADULT, CHILD - THREE EGO (SELF) STATES

Dr. Eric Berne, M.D., a famous psychiatrist, named the three people inside us *Parent* (P), *Adult* (A), and *Child* (C). The Child Ego State is that part of us which feels, has impulses, wants, likes, dislikes, is curious. It's a recorder of the feelings we have had from birth on. No matter if you are age 1, 2, 3, 14, 24, 48, or 82, you have had a variety of feelings. These feelings and impulses influence how you are going to behave right now. For example, I'm sure that if you are hungry or hurting, you don't feel like

Area of contamination

"Not being able to pay attention because your Child is feeling something, is Child-Contaminated Adult."

24

reading this book now. Too difficult to think (A) right now. My stomach (C) is growling. Later on today, when you've taken care of those Child feelings, you'll probably be better able to turn on your Adult and understand what I am talking about. But, when you are hungry, angry, hurting, or upset about something (Child), it is hard for your (Adult) to "pay attention." The Child in us is much stronger than our Parent or Adult. If you are hungry, hurting or upset, the Child messes up your Adult and you can't "think." We call that inability to think a Child-Contaminated Adult. "X" is the area in the Adult which is contaminated.

So when you are unable to think or unable to remember or concentrate, something is messing up your Adult. At that time, maybe the best thing to do is to turn your attention to your Child or to your Parent to find out what is going on. Then maybe, you can handle it better. Prejudice or bigotry (hating someone because of their race, religion, or skin color) is an example of Parent-Contaminated Adult.

"Hating someone because of their skin color is Parent-Contaminated Adult."

"NOW" IS WHEN YOU LIVE!

A third idea of TA is that NOW! RIGHT NOW! is important. There is no other time to change. No other time to think. We cannot change the past, and the future isn't here yet. We *can* change what we are doing NOW.

So, the basic ideas are, then, that we are all *born OK*; that there are three people inside of us who do our deciding, and at least two of them will sometimes mess up our ability to think; and that, when we want to do some good thinking, we had better take care of these two first, or we will not be able to do so. It can't be some other year; it can't be some other day. We must take care of Kid and Parent all the time if our Adult is to function effectively. We can only do whatever we do right now. There is no yesterday or tomorrow. I could wish, perhaps, that I had done whatever I wanted to do sooner, or hope that I am going to do it better next time, but all I can do, I must do *now*. Lots of us spend most of our lives wishing we hadn't done something or wishing we had done something we neglected to do (study, be nice to someone, save money), or we're waiting for something good to occur or being afraid of something bad. This way, we never live our lives at all. *Now* is the most important time of your life. There isn't any better time. There isn't any other time to do what you have to do. If you are going to write a book, like this, it has to be right now. It can't be some other year or some other day. *Many of us spend our lives regretting the past or fearing the future.*

TODAY IS THE TOMORROW I WORRIED ABOUT YESTERDAY

My mother, Amy Freed, always told me (Parent Tape # 4364), "Today is the tomorrow I worried about yesterday that never came." Do your best right now and that's all you can do. If you do that, you'll probably handle things pretty well. If you are going to live your life to the fullest, TA says live it NOW. This is the only moment that you have, and you have to do the very best you can with it. Sometimes, doing your best means doing nothing. Sometimes, that might be the best thing to do. Of course, we don't recommend doing nothing on a continual basis, or earning a living becomes kind of difficult.

PUZZLES, ANYONE?

Do you ever find yourself puzzled about making a decision? "Should I buy the motorcycle or a car? Should I go on the camping trip or stay home to study? Should I two-time my friend and go out with that other person? Should I make out with this new person?" Sometimes, it helps to do nothing. Put off making the decision. Later, you may find it's easier. Perhaps you will feel differently, or get additional information. When you're puzzled, you may not have all the data. One good rule to follow: If someone is trying to "sell" you something and you have to decide in a hurry, "don't buy it!" You know, like, "if you don't take it now, someone else will. It'll be gone tomorrow." An "OK! That's the risk I have to take, but I want to think about it" will keep you out of being conned into things you may regret.

THE "UNTIL" SCRIPT

Lots of people I know live their whole life *waiting until* . . . until they graduate, until they get married, until they have their baby, until their

(Part I)

"You may want to skip school and go to a concert . . . "

(Part II)

" . . . but if you flunk as a result, you may miss a whole lot of concerts."

children get through school, until they finish the building, get the job done, get a promotion, get a raise, or get a new car, or win a fortune to retire. That's when they are going to start living. And I think you can see that if you do this, you're not going to do much living at all. On the other hand, you can go to the other extreme and say, "I'm just going to live for this moment only." That doesn't take account of your safety, or other people's needs or wants. So, while living in the present is very important, making use of the present to plan for your needs in the future is also important. That is done in the Adult, now! So, know what is going on right now, and act also in

Just as soon as Junior here gets big enough
to be out on his own . . . that's when
we'll start livin' it up!

Eh? What's that Mamma? Eh?

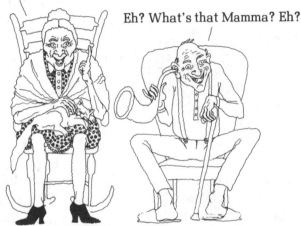

"Lots of people live their whole life waiting until . . . "

Goo!

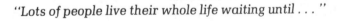

terms of what is going to happen as a result of what you are doing now. This gives you a choice of allowing your Kid out or of putting off satisfaction till a better time. For example, you may want (C) to skip school and go to a concert or fishing. No question, that's fun. On the other hand, if you don't take the test and then flunk the course as a result, you may have to take it over in the summer. If that happens, you'll miss a whole lot of fishing and other fun things.

TA teaches us that you can *change* yourself to whatever you want to be. The only time to change is right now. Lots of people delay. They say, "Well, someday when things get better . . . " and then they put off making changes. How often I've heard people say, "Well, I am going to swear off smoking tomorrow," or "I'm going to go on a diet — next week." Of course, tomorrow for them never comes, or if it does, they fail after a half-hearted effort.

TA IS A METHOD OF CHANGE FOR EVERYBODY

I've talked a little about what TA theory is, and something about its philosophy. TA is also a method to change the things in ourselves that we find uncomfortable. Physicians, psychiatrists, psychologists, social workers, and school counselors use TA to help people with special problems like nervousness or serious mental disturbances. But TA has a much broader use.

TA IS FOR EVERYBODY

I believe TA is for everybody. When everybody uses it, people won't get so nervous and upset. Schools and churches are teaching TA. TA is now a body of knowledge, written down in books in an increasingly more accurate language. In this sense, it approaches being a science as well as a theory, philosophy, and therapy. Current research is beginning to test its ideas and to demonstrate that it works for many people.

You don't have to be disturbed or have a dilemma in order to use TA to understand yourself or others better. If you are old enough to be puzzled about what you do and why you do it, you can use TA to help figure yourself out. There are many things that you probably could do better for yourself and the people you care about if you knew how.

People used to tell me that I was my own worst enemy, but nobody ever told me how to change. So, I went on being my own worst enemy until I ran into TA. Now I'm becoming my own best friend. Of course, it is harder for me to change at my age than it would be for you. But I've been making some changes in me. I understand myself and other people better. And that's what this book is all about. To help you to know yourself, to know who in you is talking or acting NOW, and to help you to change if you want to. So, TA is a theory of personality (P,A,C) which tells us we're OK. TA is a way of understanding ourselves and others. TA is a philosophy (I'm OK, You're OK). Most important, TA is a method of working with other peole to solve individual life puzzles. In group you can test out your ideas and your feelings and get straight answers. TA leads to your learning to talk straighter and to make more sense to others. Some people think it could be used well by our political leaders to solve the problems of nations of the world. (Tom Harris once said, "I want to take TA to Moscow." I want to take it everywhere — like to Sacramento, Washington D.C., the United Nations, the Middle East, to Ireland and Africa.)

QUESTIONS FOR YOUR ADULT

1. What is a Transaction?
2. What is a stroke? Why should you care or know about strokes? How will it help you?
3. What does OK mean? Are you OK? Do you feel OK? If not what can you do to feel OK? If not what can you do to change?
4. Why does Tom Harris want to take TA to Moscow?

EXERCISES

1. Practice giving strokes to classmates. Give someone you like a polite compliment.
2. Lightly touch (2 seconds) 10 different people each day (let your Parent tell you where to touch them so your Kid doesn't get clobbered). Shake hands, pat shoulder, massage somebody's neck.
3. Give Mom or Dad a back rub. Get one too.
4. Focus in on your present (right now.) What are you feeling? (Anger, hurt, afraid, sexy, hungry, worried, puzzled.)
5. If you're up-tight take a deep breath — close your eyes, now relax. Do this twice. Feel better? Good.

PROBLEMS FOR THOUGHT AND DISCUSSION

1. What are your prejudices? Where did you learn them? Do they fit the person whom you know? Can you change your prejudices?
2. Write out several transactions and analyze them by drawing arrows (as described earlier in this chapter) to show where each person is coming from.

IDEAS AND WORDS TO LEARN MORE ABOUT

1. Transaction
2. Strokes
3. "I" statements
4. Parent, Adult, Child
5. Contaminated Adult

Chapter III

STRAIGHT TALK

"A suspicious parent makes an artful child."   Haliburton

Over and over, teens complain to me about the difficulty they have in getting along with "people." They say they like people, but they don't know how to get along with them. The people they find hardest to get along with, they say, are the people in their own family, teachers, kids in school, and people with whom they work.

Whether young, like you, or old like me, each of us has to deal with people. All my life, I too have found this a very difficult task. I have found it hard to understand other people, to know how to cope with them. If I "stand up" for myself I come on too strong. If I don't, I allow them to walk on me. I'm told I am, therefore, a passive - aggressive personality. Some people feel they have to do everything right - we call them perfectionists or compulsive personalities. But names don't seem to be much help, do they? What you and I want to know is how to get along better with ourselves and other people.

HOW TO WIN PIC'S AND INFLUENCE BROTHERS AND SISTERS

Do you want to get along better with your folks, your younger brother or sister, maybe even grandmother, grandfather, big brother, sister? Do you want to get out of mad talk with your friend and be more *effective?* You do? I can tell you how. Learn to talk straight to them, without angles, games, lies, or cons. Very often we don't know that we're coming on crooked. TA will help you find out. In fact, you are doing very well in finding out when you are coming on Parent (P), Adult (A), Child (C). In doing so, you probably have found out about other people a little bit: where they come on from. I guess you also found out that if you make like a Child, they will talk to you from their Parent, and you don't get along very well.

Example: Remember how you feel when it's almost dinner time and you want to eat — anything! You ask for a cookie, or piece of bread, or a sandwich. Mother or Dad says "You can wait. You'll spoil your dinner if you eat now." The "you can wait" discounts you and your feeling of hunger and says, "Don't feel the way you feel." It also says wait and enjoy your dinner so I can enjoy your enjoyment. Look at how hard we've worked to prepare you a good meal. You then respond with your discount, "I don't want to wait. I'm hungry now — can't you hear how hungry I am? I don't care if I spoil your fun in my enjoyment." This looks like this:

Cross transactions can be put downs.

You feel as if you're being *put down* when somebody's Parent talks to you. You feel irritated, annoyed, used, and that's probably what is going on.

CRISIS TALK IS S-A-D

One trouble in getting along with others is that we are not straight with ourselves. We have talked in TA about being straight, or of having our head together, and so on. We get into hot water with important people around us, because of three things we do. This is *SAD, [and here's why]*. Begin with the letters which spell SAD. We can remember them, because the initials are S,A,D. Number 1 (S). Sulking is talking to ourselves, angrily and silently, because we are afraid that we can't talk back to the people in power with whom we are angry. So, we *Sulk* (S), and we are *Silent* (S), and we keep our anger inside and wait to attack. Dr. Pemberton[3] calls us the "Anger Inners." Number 2 (A): We *attack* (A) someone. Number two'ers are "Anger Outers." When we attack, we tell others how wrong they are, blame them for their shortcomings, defend ourselves, and label them. This feels good, but it makes them (1) Silent and (2) Angry. Then *they* wait to (2) Attack (A) back. So, we do a 1-2, 1-2 until we're into a fight or a quit. And the conversation may go something like this: "Well, if it wasn't for you." (defense) "It's all your fault." (blame) "Look what you got me into." "You're dumb." (label) "You shouldn't have done that." "I didn't do it!" (defense) "You are just saying I did, to get out of . . . ," "You're a liar" (label), and so on. These kinds of conversations lead to building up more and more anger. More and more ill feeling and hurt on both sides. We play the blame game.

MOVE NUMBER THREE — DECEIT (D)

Then we may move into play #3, which is Deceitful (D) behavior. For example, sarcasm. "I suppose you'd just like me to do everything *you* say," or, "OK, so then I'm supposed to obey you without question, is that it?" and so on. In (D), we frequently feel one thing and say another. Or say an awful (I could kill myself) and laugh. When we are hurt or angry, we may cover it with a straight face or a smile. So, there we have the SAD way to talk to someone. The three steps to interpersonal *crisis*.

34

Here's a summary:
Doing the Sad One-Two-Three Step: When having a crisis you may do one or more of the following:

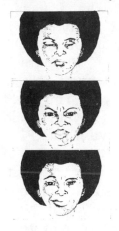

S 1 - Sullen Silence (S)
You go sullen and silent and wait for a chance to explode.

A 2 - Attack (A)
You leap out and attack someone - blame them - defend yourself, or call them a name (label them) dumb, stupid, monster, rotten kid, brat, etc.

D 3 - Deceive them (D)
You become sarcastic (say one thing and mean something else), or "put on a good face." Feel one thing and say or behave another. Play games (If it weren't for you, Poor me.)

That spells SAD, and it's a sad way to behave because you lose the love of your friend or relative and wind up with bad feelings for both of you.

FOUR-FIVE-SIX, OR HOW TO GET IT FIXED

The first step in feeling better about others begins with feeling good about you. *You are OK!* So, tell yourself this frequently. You are important. You're worth a great deal, and you can think. You may do destructive things, goof up, blow it, or whatever, but you are "OK". If you want to change, you can if you will. You're OK not to change, too. The first step is to start loving yourself. If you don't, who else will? This is different from what you have been doing. It's different from what you've been "taught." It's entirely different. Assert your self worth. Share your wins as well as your losses. That's not bragging, it's being pleased with your success. And I'll tell you something else. *You can do it, not only at home,* but you can also do it at school. You can do it when you are having fun — wherever you are. Like, when you are out on a date, or when you are in trouble, maybe even when you are getting busted, you can love yourself. Hopefully, you won't get busted, but it may even help then if you are. You sure need a "best friend" when things go wrong. What you don't need is someone to criticize you and tell you what you should have done.

ONE, TWO, THREE VERSUS FOUR, FIVE, SIX

When somebody chews you out, or does something mean to you now, you probably call him/her a name, talk back, go silent, or try to get even with him/her. You may mumble to yourself things you'd like to do or say to them (sullen silence). Sometimes it isn't politic to tell "them" off. You feel like it, though. Right? You feel like hurting them like they are hurting you. What you are doing is discounting them. You're probably thinking, "They don't care about my feelings, so why should I care about their feelings?" But, you're not counting your own feelings, because you don't know what your own feelings are. Now, here is a way to get out of that.

I COUNT! WHERE AM I?

First, tell yourself, "I count because I exist." Second, "My feelings count. Now, who should they count with more than with me?" So, what I suggest you do is *talk to yourself*. Let your Child talk to your Parent. Nutty, huh? It used to be that when people talked to themselves, they were thought to be on their way to the funny farm. (We've learned that talking to yourself about your own feelings is a healthy thing to do.) If you *don't* talk to yourself, how can you check out what's happening inside of you? You won't know what your feelings are, and your feelings are you. If your Child (feelings) is hurting, angry or afraid, you need strokes. So, I want *you* (P) to take care of your Child. How about that? I want you to start being a protective, kindly, loving person (Parent) to yourself. Here's how you do it.

(4) *Stop! Listen to your Child!* The first thing you do is say, from your child, "Hey I count!" Then, "What am I feeling?" asks your Adult. Now your Adult listens and your nurturing Parent listens. Suppose your brother has ratted (told) on you. Your Child is angry. "I'm so angry I could spit in his face. I want to tell him off. I hate him. I could just bash his stupid face in. I'm angrrry!" Then, "I'm also hurt that he would tell on me after all the times I've helped him. And he looked at my letters, the sneak. Then he told mom. Ohh! I'm so angry and HURT." Now shift from your Child to your Adult and get some information. "Why did he do it? I'll ask him and see if what he says makes sense to me. I'll listen!" So your Adult listens and hears him, and so instead of pulling an attack you can then switch to (6a) i.e. "Where is brother? Right now? What is he feeling?" (and so on).

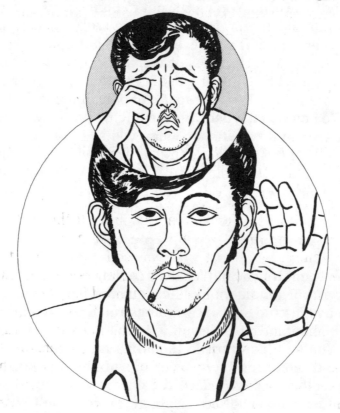

"Stop, Listen to your Child."

WHERE IS HE?

So (5) instead of denying your feelings, listen to them. Then (6a) you switch! Switch to "Where is brother? What is he feeling?" *Not* what is he saying? *Not* what he did, *not* the way he is acting, but *what is he feeling?* OK? Now, you have to use your head (Adult). You have to figure this out or guess what he is feeling. So, think to yourself, "Well, maybe he is as angry as I am. I wonder what I did to help him get angry. Anyway, he is angry and maybe *he* feels *hurt* about something. Maybe he is disappointed he didn't get to go to the ball game. I know he didn't get to go. He had to stay home and take care of the lawn. Maybe he is unhappy about that." OK?

SPECULATE! THEN, TELL THEM WHAT THEY FEEL

Now, that's what you figure out, or as we call it *"speculate"* or guess about your brother's feelings. So, the next step is very easy. (6b) You simply *say to him what you have just been thinking. Start it with a "you" message* like this, "You are pretty angry and unhappy about havi g to stay home and not get to go to the ball game." And you say it just about the way I said it. Not in a mothering way. Not in a making fun of way. Not in an I feel sorry for you way. *Just tell him what he feels.* Then watch what happens. You will see a whole change in the way he comes on with you, and *you'll feel different.*

What I just illustrated for you is how you can begin to make use of TA at home, in school, or anywhere. Begin to tune in on where people are, where they are coming from. See if they are coming on from their Parent. Adult, or Child. Then find out where you are — you're important. If you are in your Child and the other person is in the Parent, it helps to know that. If you don't, you will have a cross transaction and cause a further break between you. Cross transactions lead to fights, sullen silence, and loss of love, friendship, or respect.

THERE'S NO TALK WITHOUT LISTENING

If you don't hear what the other person is saying, and you don't know what he is feeling, then what you say doesn't make any sense to him. You don't get together. You stay angry. So, once more, here's the way to make use of TA at home with brothers and sisters, mothers and fathers, grandmothers, grandfathers, uncles, aunts, and all the rest of them. First of all (4) Get more information — really listen. Then (5) Find out where you are: What am I feeling? Be honest with yourself. Figure it out. It only takes a second or two. Then think (6) "Where are *they* coming from?" First you, yourself, then them. Then, if you have *speculated* (6a) about "where" they are (6b), *tell them!* Be honest (authentic) with them! When you tell them what they are feeling and they agree, you will see a big change come over them. I'll bet you. I bet they will look at you with amazement. The first time you do this, they will think in wonder, "I can't believe this. She (he) heard me! She (he) knows what I am feeling and cares." Use *"you"* messages like this: *"you're angry," "you're sad," "you're upset," "you didn't like."* etc.

Now, you'll see! This will work fine. They will probably say, "Yes, I am upset. I am angry with you and I am trying to tell you that." Then what do you do? A thing called "active listening." If you want more clues about how to handle this, go to a book written by a fellow named Thomas Gordon. It is called *Parent Effectiveness Training [P.E.T.]*. In P.E.T., he is talking about mothers and fathers. But, it really doesn't matter. Young or old, we all function the same way. We elders have had more practice (in goofing things up, too). Just like TA is always the same, — regardless of whether you are in school, at home, on a date, in trouble, wherever it is — TA is always the same. And you are always going to be the same unless you learn how to be different. That's what you're doing now.

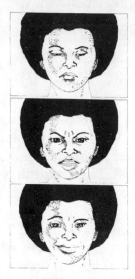

How to have a SAD fight is:

1 - Sullen silence
    (Mumble to self)

2 - Attack - blame, advise,
    defend self, call names.

3 - Deceit - say one thing
    and mean another
    play games.

How to be more effective and get along better:

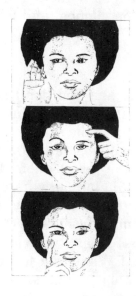

4 - LISTEN - get more information

5 - Hear yourself - be honest
    with yourself.

6a - Guess (speculate) about
     other's feelings.

6b - Paraphrase. Tell them
     "You are feeling . . ." Be
     honest with them.

When you come on 6b, you are authentic to your friend. Then he or she will register "five" and be able to do a "six" with you. In this way, both of you can be honest with yourself and the other person. Here's the way it looks:

	Ego State	Transactions
Crisis talk	C	1 - Sulk: "Yeah I get all the blame. He/she never blames her/himself."
	C	2 - Attack: "It's all your/his/her fault. She's/he's a rotten stinker."
	C	3 - Deceit: "No, I don't mind (I sure do)."
Human Effectiveness	A	4 - Get info: "What's his gripe?"
	C	5 - Feel me (truth) "I'm angry."
	A	6a - Feel him/her. "He's angry and upset."
	A	b - Tell him/her. "You're angry and upset."

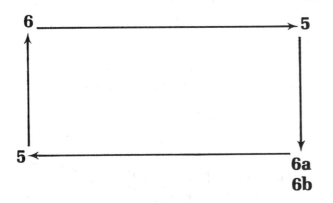

Start here: Be aware of your own feelings.

Authentic transactions lead to understanding and problem solving.

QUESTIONS FOR YOUR ADULT

1. How can you get along better with your friends?
2. What is the SAD method of talking which leads to a crisis in your relationship?
3. What is a better way to get along with friends and other important people? Talk about the 4-5-6 method.

EXERCISES

1. Practice tuning in on your own feelings (anger, hurt, sad, happy). What is going on? How can you change the way you feel, right now? Will you do it?
2. You would like to get along better at home. Right? Do this one. Next time brother or dad or mother looks happy, tell them that. Say, "You feel pretty good". Or, if they are reading a book, you might say, "That book looks like it's fun to read." Don't always pick on the bad feelings to "reflect." It's great to be able to share your fun feelings with someone else. So, when they are having fun, watch for their looking happy, and then tell them that. But first, before you do that, *remember to find out where you are.* You may be feeling down, you may not be feeling happy. Tell yourself that, "I'm not very happy today. I feel kind of unhappy, disinterested, and so on." Then tell *them* what they are feeling and watch their expression change. Then write and tell me what happened. I really want to know.
3. Follow the summary on the previous page, filling in your own words and phrases. Practice on paper — or talking out loud to yourself and then try it with someone in your family to avoid a crisis.

IDEAS AND WORDS TO LEARN MORE ABOUT

1. Passive
2. Aggressive
3. Put downs
4. Straight talk
5. Assertiveness
6. Cross transactions
7. Paraphrase

Chapter IV

WARM FUZZIES AND COLD PRICKLIES AROUND THE CLOCK

(HOW WE USE OUR TIME TO GET STROKES)

*"One real stroke is worth a
thousand reassurances."   Al Freed*

HOW DO YOU USE YOUR 24 HOURS?

When I was talking to you in Chapter I about strokes, I said that it was very, important that each of us get strokes. Strokes keep us alive. Strokes are actions (touches, smiles, words, frowns, applause, hits, praise, approval) by others which make us feel. They are as necessary as food and water. We must have strokes to live.

Our skin is the largest sense organ of our body. The skin needs strokes to be healthy. We must get them from other people, and we must learn to give them so that others may live. This exchange of strokes is called a transaction. Strokes, as we have said earlier, can be either physical (touches), or psychological (approval, visual, smiles, nods, praise, etc.) They can be pleasant or unpleasant. When someone touches you, that's a physical stroke. If it feels good, it's a positive or pleasant stroke - a warm fuzzy. If it feels bad, hurts, or jars us, it's a negative stroke - a cold prickly.

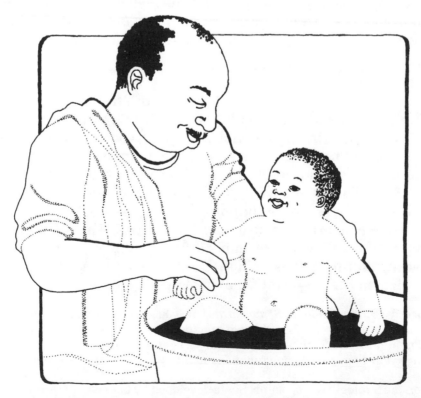

"If it feels good, it's a positive or pleasant stroke — a Warm Fuzzy."

You get strokes when people tell or do unpleasant things to you. Compliments, smiles, praise, encouragement or needles, put downs. rejections, criticism (get on your case), punishment, sarcasm are strokes.

In any case, nice or not, strokes are important. They are so important that all of us spend most of our waking and sleeping time doing things to get them. Now, how do people go about getting strokes? How do you get them? And, what do you do when you get them? Do you take 'em and enjoy 'em, or do you "Paint them brown" with an "Aw shucks, warn't nothin'?"

THE PLAY IS THE THING

Dr. Berne, in his book *Games People Play*, and later in his book *What Do You Say After You Say Hello?*, describes six main ways that people have to get strokes. I have added a seventh. These ways use up all of our 24 hours a day. Here they are: 1) Withdrawal; 2) Ritual; 3) Pastimes; 4) Activities; 5) Games; 6) Fun; 7) Intimacy. Which ones do you use the most? Are you satisfied? If not, you can change and feel better. You may not notice it, but you'll find that the order in which I present these is related to the degree of closeness each brings you to other people. Withdrawal, the first and least satisfying, separates you the most from other people and feels safest. Intimacy, the last and most satisfying, brings you closest to people and is most risky. The "safer" you are, the less intense the strokes, the longer it takes to satisfy you. Thus, you use more time. Compare day dreaming with work activities for time. In the same way, the farther away you are from people, the safer you feel, but the less satisfying are the strokes you get. So, you see, if you've been feeling lonely, unhappy, or depressed, maybe you've been selecting ways of getting strokes that aren't as satisfying as you need. If this is so, make a change in your choice of time structuring and stroke-getting behavior.

SUBJECTIVE STROKE SCALE (SSS)*

In order for you to get the kind and amount of strokes you need for a satisfying life you'll need to know how you are getting strokes now. Take a look at the Subjective Stroke Scale (shown). Can you begin to guess how many strokes you get under each heading? You may find it useful to try to keep a record of the kinds of things you do each day and then make yourself a SSS. At the end of a week you'll have a good idea of how you are getting strokes. If you're not as happy as you'd like to be, perhaps you can increase one or more time structuring activities. This will mean that you will do less of another. For example if you want more "FUN" you may have to give up Rapping (Pastiming). Try it out and see how it works. There's no right pattern — just what feels good to you.

> "The Subjective Stroke Scale (SSS) measures how you get your Strokes. How do you use your time to get Strokes? Is this satisfactory to you? If not, what must you change? Fill in a Stroke Scale each day until you get a picture of your stroke life. Then change your time-structuring functions so that you feel more satisfied."

*Based on the Subjective Discomfort Scale developed by Sherwin Cotter and Jose Guerra in the book *Assertion Training*, 1976.

44

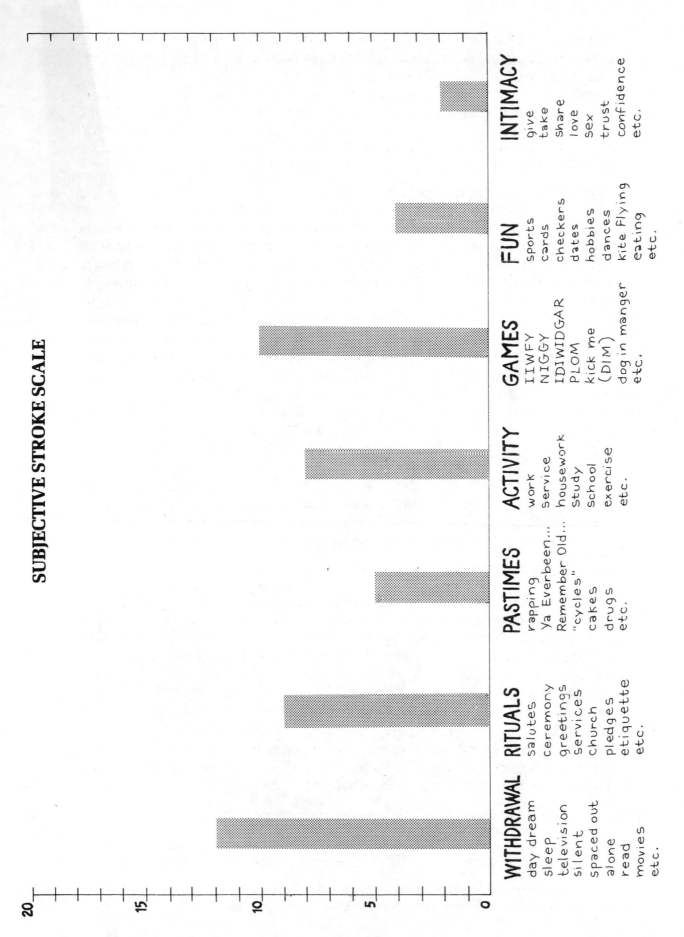

SUBJECTIVE STROKE SCALE

WITHDRAWAL	RITUALS	PASTIMES	ACTIVITY	GAMES	FUN	INTIMACY
day dream	salutes	rapping	work	IIWFY	sports	give
sleep	ceremony	Ya Everbeen...	service	NIGY	cards	take
television	greetings	Remember Old...	housework	IDIWIDGAR	checkers	share
silent	services	"cycles"	study	PLOM	dates	love
spaced out	church	cakes	school	kick me	hobbies	sex
alone	pledges	drugs	exercise	(DIM)	dances	trust
read	etiquette	etc.	etc.	dog in manger	kite flying	confidence
movies	etc.			etc.	eating	etc.
etc.					etc.	

20 15 10 5 0

WITHDRAWAL

Sometimes, when we don't find enough satisfaction in the way we are living, we tend to go inside ourselves to find strokes. Some people use drugs to do this. Berne calls this Withdrawal. Withdrawal is the least involving with other people. Withdrawal, as the name suggests, occurs when we attempt to get strokes for ourselves while we are alone - physically or mentally.

During physical withdrawal, you may go to your room and lie on your bed, daydream, read a book, or go to sleep. During mental withdrawal, in the presence of others, you may day dream, allow your mind to wander to things you'd rather be doing (like in class when you think of playing a game or fishing or romancing a cute guy or gal). TV and movies are ways of getting strokes while "alone." We identify (feel like the hero is me) with the leading character and experience his or her feelings, accept the pain or

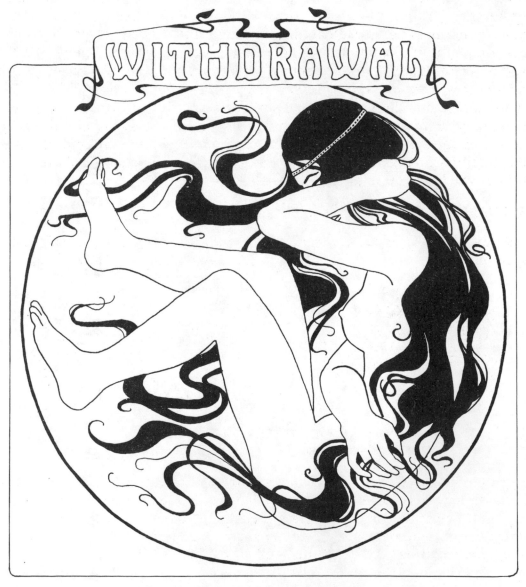

"Withdrawal occurs when we attempt to get strokes for ourselves while we are alone."

pleasure he or she is experiencing. We may dream of great accomplishments, of great inventions or ideas for making a lot of money. Actually, many of the great inventions or greatest books result from daydreaming. Of course, to make such withdrawal productive, we have to follow it with lots of work — like writing the book or building the invention, or starting the business.

Withdrawal involves us least with people-in-the-flesh, and most with people-in-our-dreams (fantasy, imagination). It's a one-way transaction — from screen-to-me, book-to-me, TV-to-me, or just me-to-me (dream). It's safe, but not very satisfying. The creative part of us is in our Child, but our daydreams must be made real by our Adult if they are to have lasting value.

THE LITTLE PROFESSOR

The creative part of us is in our Child and is called "The Little Professor." The Little Professor is the Adult in the Child. But, our daydreams must be worked out by our Adult and made real, or all dreams remain just that. Sometimes we daydream, with or without the help of TV, radio, or a book. We attempt to find our satisfactions through the adventures, happiness, and excitement of other people. Some of this is OK. It stimulates our thinking and leads to personal success. But, if we get our kicks only out of dreams (daydreams), we soon find ourselves either getting bored, or getting further and further away from what's real, and that isn't the healthiest way to get your strokes. Besides, it takes us away from things which pay off in people strokes.

RITUALS

A Ritual is a way society says to behave. It is a commonly-agreed-upon way of acting; a set of rules which gets you strokes. "Hello, Hi. Good

"Rituals are the way society says to do things.
Do them wrong, and you get rejected."

morning, Please, May I, and Thanks," are Rituals. A ritual is limited to a series of simple transactions. Our Pledge of Allegiance is a good example of a ritual. Every time you have repeated the "Pledge of Allegiance," sung "the Star-Spangled Banner," said a prayer, taken part in a church service, a wedding ceremony, or saluted an officer or the flag, you have been participating in a Ritual. Rituals are ways society says to do things. If you do them right, you get strokes. Do them wrong, and you get rejected. They are the second "safest" way to get strokes.

Rituals come in two flavors: formal and informal. The formal kind are written down and must be followed precisely as prescribed — they are rules about how to behave. Some of you who go to church know that when you walk into the church, you do certain things which you've been taught to do. In some churches, people bow, in others they kneel, make hand signs, put their hands in water, or say "Gut Shabbas (Good Sabbath)." The usher at a wedding follows a ritual: he greets guests in a certain way, holds his bent arm for the lady, and conducts her to a seat (on the bride's side or the groom's). Have you heard of the *Book of Etiquette* by Emily Post? She was an authority on rituals for many years, and taught us "manners", especially when we ate. Hers was a book of Rituals.

Greetings may be formal or informal Rituals. They are determined by your society. If done correctly, they are ways of getting us strokes. Informal Rituals, at the right time, with the right person, get you strokes. With the wrong person, they may get you cold pricklies. When you come to school, you may greet your friends by saying "Hi" and getting back a stroke when you say "Hi" to you. "Hi" is an informal Ritual. How can you get more strokes in school? Right! Give more!

If you use a formal greeting, it could be a "cold prickly" to someone you're close to. For example, "Good morning, Beane," to a friend who had stood you up earlier in the week could be a message, "Look, you're not my friend anymore." In this case, you would have given two cold strokes. (1) Calling the friend by the last name, and (2) saying good morning very formally instead of your usual "Hi, Joe." Then he would return two similar strokes to you by responding with your name and the formal good morning. Think about that formal Ritual of "Good morning." It doesn't mean too much, except that, "back in the olden days," people were wishing each other a good morning. Now, we're saying, "Have a nice day," (H-A-N-D), and that's the same kind of thing. On the other hand, if we give an informal greeting to the boss, we may get fired, unless we have an informal relationship with him or her. When we applaud, we're giving a "hand." When we help people, we're doing the same thing. Hands give strokes. If we give a stroke, we expect to get one. Think how you feel when you say, "Hi, Joan," and she doesn't answer you. You feel shorted, right? No return strokes. Society has set up a lot of rituals like this. For instance, we have rituals on the telephone. Some people say, "Good morning, this is Cuss Company." Other people say, "Hi! It's your nickel! Start talking!" In any case, we have Rituals by which we give strokes and get strokes.

PASTIMES

Then there are Pastimes. Berne defined a Pastime as a "series of half-ritual, simple transactions about a single topic to fill in time." These are not the usual fun things, like playing baseball, going skating, or rapping with your buddies. We'll talk about them later. A Pastime is a programmed, predictable exchange of strokes between two or more people about one certain subject. You almost know in advance what will be said. You engage in Pastimes, for instance, when you talk about what's wrong with school, teachers (yeuch!), parents, brothers, sisters, my girl friend

PASTIMING

"A pastime is a programmed, predictable exchange of strokes between people."

(boy friend), motorcycles, football, cake baking, clothes, and so on. Fun talk about, "Did you see the new Harley that just came out?" is a Pastime. Then you may continue to talk about cycles for awhile, each of you telling what you know about different kinds of cycles — Indians, Harleys, choppers — and so on. In a way, each of you is getting a feeling of OKness out of showing the other your knowledge of cycles. Gossip is a Pastime. "Did you hear about Bill and Jane?" Sometimes, Pastimes are about what's "wrong with parents" or "parents always" or "teachers always." You may talk about whether marijuana should be legalized, or "I think there ought to be a law against . . ." Maybe, it's how to run a bluff against trips showing in a seven card poker game. Thus, we fill in (structure) time, and get strokes just for being around somebody else who agrees with, or maybe disagrees with you. Some other well known, easily recognized Pastimes are, "Weather"; "Y'ever been"; "Do you remember old . . . ", etc. In any case, the strokes we get from Pastimes are OK and they help us get closer, better acquainted, without getting too close too soon. But if we get *only those*, after awhile, we get bored. They're not too satisfying, but they're better than Withdrawal. They bring you a little closer to people (See Stroke Scale). Thus, they are less safe, but more satisfying than Withdrawal.

"Activities are high Stroke producers."

ACTIVITY

Next is Activity. Work or school are examples of Activities which get us many strokes. It matters little, really, if we go to school, work at home or in an office, for pay or not. If somebody likes what we do, we get a feeling that we're OK. We like to do work where we get paid. But, we love to work for a boss who says, "Good job." We may do our school work and be satisfied by a good grade. But, we love teachers who somehow let us know they think we are OK with them. Lots of people hate their jobs or school or home because nobody tells them they're doing OK. One of the reasons we may not like school is because, when we work hard at studies, we don't always get strokes. Most of us don't get top grades. When we don't get good grades, we're not getting plus strokes. So, we soon get tired of "trying," and yearn for the time when we "can get out of all this and go to work." We daydream that that is where it's at. We'll get paid, and be liked. The boss will really appreciate us for the things that we do. Or, "I'll just go on welfare and never have to do nothin' I don't want to do." Can you think of other activities? Activities are high stroke producers. That's why we spend so much time (8-12 hours a day) on them. They are not as safe as pastimes. We're more open to criticism. They bring us closer to people.

I've mentioned a number of ways people spend time getting strokes. We get them while involved in Withdrawal (daydreams), Rituals, Pastimes, work (Activities). There are three other ways: Games, Fun, and the last, Intimacy.

GAMES

Dr. Claude Steiner wrote a pamphlet called *TA Made Simple*, and you might want to read that sometime. He says Games are crooked, hidden ways of getting strokes. Unlike when we play athletic games, or when we play tricks on people, *we do not know that we are playing Games.* We use Games to get strokes that we don't think we're entitled to. For instance, if I feel that I'm not OK, it is because I decided a long time ago, when I was little, that if people knew what a "rotten kid" I was inside, nobody would like me. So, I'll act like I'm OK and con people into giving me strokes. For example, I'll make-believe that it's somebody else's fault if I do something wrong. Or, I'll say, "Well, if it wasn't for him . . . ."

Games are ways of getting strokes when we dont think we can get them any other way. So, we've got to con or trick people into giving us strokes. You can recognize some of the famous Games that other people use by listening for phrases like: "What'll I do? Why don't you . . . Yes, but . . . ," and "If it wasn't for you . . . " and "Mine's better than yours," and "It's all your fault," and "Look what you got me into now." Keep your ears open, and see if you can hear people using some of these gamey phrases that you've heard over and over. Finally, Jan Fling (age 19), who is reading my book critically, reminds me to stress that *everyone plays Games*, but that hard Games can be tragic. The way to get out of Games is to find out which ones you play and what you're getting from them. If it's "trouble", maybe you can quit playing.

A Game is a set of hidden transactions which occur over and over and usually wind up the same way (see *Games People Play*). Games usually have the same result (Pay off) and the end is predictable. If you find yourself going through a similar set of behaviors with the same or different people, and things always wind up badly for you, maybe you're playing a TA Game. Most of us do until we learn how to quit and come on straight.

FUN

Fun is a way of spending time getting strokes. Berne didn't mention it, and I'm puzzled about that, because he loved fun, was famous for his

"Fun is a way of spending time getting strokes."

leadership in fun things. He enjoyed jumpin' up and down parties, had a drum-set in his house for fun, and taught us how important fun is for life and health. I define fun as a deliberate and intentional way of spending time, purely to get strokes. When the thing you're doing is no longer fun, you can quit. Like sandlot football or baseball, bathing in the ocean, dancing, playing poker (one of Berne's favorite fun things), dating, playing checkers, tennis, bowling, skiing, etc. All are for fun, a legitimate and essential set of time structuring functions which get us high levels of stroking, with low risk and high closeness. The American public pays more money for fun than any other single commodity. (Stars of stage, screen, TV, and radio receive exorbitant salaries if they provide fun.) Fun strokes can be gotten from any time structuring function, but only in Fun Functions do we engage "just for Fun."

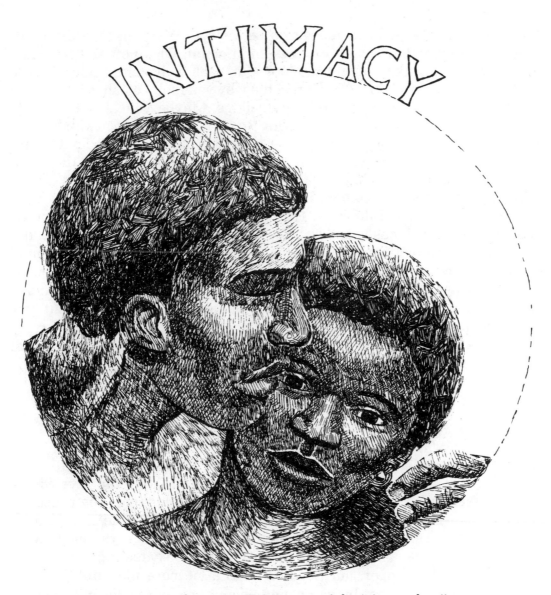

"Intimacy is the most satisfying way of obtaining strokes."

INTIMACY

Finally, there's Intimacy. Intimacy is the most intense, satisfying way of obtaining strokes. Unfortunately, Intimacy is not as available to most people as we would like it to be. People seldom use this direct, powerful, physical, and psychological exchange of strokes. Probably this is because. when we are little, we're told not to get too close. We're told not to touch; not to let other people touch us; not to get too close to our Mother, Dad, brother or sister, nor to strangers, and so on. "Don't touch," "don't stare," "don't look" are constant guides. We're also told not to show our feelings.

Intimacy is based on the idea "I'm OK — You're OK" (see T. Harris reference); that we can be closer to each other and not hurt each other. Intimacy allows us to *give ourselves away*, to come on straight and honest and say the things we're thinking and feeling without being afraid of a put-down or a discount (see cartoon). Did you ever feel really mad?

53

Somebody says, "You have no right to be angry!" Well, that's a discount! When someone tells you your feelings don't count. Or, another time when you've said you were unhappy and looked it, somebody said, "Don't frown. Smile." They were saying, "Don't feel the way you feel. Look happy so I can feel better." They didn't count your feelings. Maybe you've said that to somebody. You probably were trying to "cheer 'em up." Maybe you weren't counting their feelings. So, our book is to help you to find out where you are, and where other people are, so that you can be closer to them and achieve a degree of Intimacy that will be satisfying.

To repeat, we spend 24 hours a day attempting to get strokes because strokes keep us alive. I think it's pretty important you find out how you do it. Some people do it easily and happily, and other people do it in a way that keeps them from getting strokes. This is very annoying to people around them. They go through life unhappy, bewildered, feeling "nobody loves me." Most people don't want to be annoying to other people, especially because they like positive strokes. Maybe this will help you to find out how to get them without being a pain in the neck. But, I could be wrong. Sometimes people who think they can't get good strokes become good at getting unpleasant strokes. If you do that and want to change, you can. You are not doomed by fate to "Unhappyville." *Change your point of view* and your whole life will change.

INTIMACY AND SEX

Intimacy sometimes involves sexy feelings which we are frequently told not to have until we get married. Of course, we all know that everybody *has* sexy feelings, but we're seldom told how to handle them. The reason is mostly because, until recently, very few PIC's felt comfortable enough with their own sexy feelings to talk to you about them. Later on in the book, we'll talk about some ways to handle your sexy feelings. Sexy feelings are just as real and useful as anger, hurt, or fear, and a lot more pleasant. But, for now, let me only say that Intimacy may involve sex, but it doesn't have to. We can be intimate with people without sex, and sex may be part of Intimacy. This is where a lot of people get mixed up. They confuse sexy feelings with Intimacy and love.

I mentioned Dr. Steiner earlier. He wrote a wonderful story called *A Fuzzy Tale* about why everybody is short on strokes. The story is so good that I've ask his permission to share it with you. Since he is a generous person, he said "OK". You'll find it at the end of this chapter. Incidentally, he invented the terms "Warm Fuzzy" and "Cold Prickly" and introduced them in this story.

RACKETS

A con man working a racket tries to make other people do what he wants them to do through threat of violence. TA Rackets are the same. For instance, love, i.e., "I won't love you if you don't eat your oatmeal." Here the person speaking is using love as a blackmail. "If you don't do it, I'll punish you," or, "I'll make you wish you had." Thus, we may use threat as

"Racket is the use of our feelings to get other people to do what we want."

If you really loved me, Archibald...

a blackmail Racket. Here we use fear to force people to do what we want. So, a Racket is the use of our feelings to get other people to do what we want. Sort of emotional blackmail. Manipulation. We usually learn our family Rackets early and then go around looking for places to use them. There are "sick headache" Rackets, depression Rackets, "nervous," angry, hurt feelings, and fear Rackets. Do you work any of these?

SCRIPTS

Most important in TA is our understanding of Life Scripts.* Muriel James talks about this a great deal in *Born to Win*, a wonderful TA book for people in high school. Claude Steiner's book, *Scripts People Live*, is equally helpful.

A Script is a life plan or a prediction made to you about your future. "You'll grow up to be . . . " or "You're just like your (Father, mother, Aunt Gleek, Uncle Smerk - and they're never any good.)" You may *think* people have told you *you have to follow* this plan. Frequently, you hear somebody say, "Well, I'm fated to this" or "Well, that's the way it has to be as far as I'm concerned because that's my life." *Well, any time you want to change, you can.* Dr. Thomas A. Harris has said that you're not responsible for what happened to you up to now, but you are responsible for what happens to you from now on. You don't have to follow a Script. You can make your own life plan. Some people say to a youngster, "When you get bit you'll be nothing but a bum. You're a born loser." This is not true! You are *not* a born loser; you are not a "born" anything except a Prinz. When you're born, *you are OK*. "But I don't feel OK!" you may say. Well, join the great throng. Most of us have Not OK feelings about ourselves because of our early set of experiences. But we are OK and we are winners. Scripts are like being tied to a certain course of action. You have to follow it. If you want to change your Script to a plan of your own, learn where you are coming on from (P,A,C). I knew two brothers, ages 15 and 17, who, because they were deserted at ages 3 and 4 by their parents, were still getting back at all "grownups" by "doing the opposite." They planned to go to jail by 18 to "show them." Sad, but silly. (They did, too.) TA is intended to help you to change the things in everyday life you want to change and to go after what you want for you now and in the future. *Now is important.* To change *now* means that you have to stop long enough to know what is going on and then choose what happens.

The rest of this book is going to be about changing. Later, we talk about using TA on dates, or when driving a car, or when playing ball, or whatever. We are going to suggest ways to use TA to do better the many different things that you do each day. So, you can, perhaps, come out feeling better about yourself and the important people in your lives — those people you meet and greet every day.

---

*Life Script is an extremely helpful TA idea discovered and explained first by Dr. Claude Steiner. He received the International Transactional Analysis Association Scientific award of the year for this.

A FUZZYTALE

Claude M. Steiner, Ph.D.*

Once upon a time, a long time ago, there lived two very happy people called Tim and Maggie with two children called John and Lucy. To understand how happy they were, you have to understand how things were in those days. You see, in those happy days everyone was given at birth a small, soft, Fuzzy Bag. Any time a person reached into this bag he was able to pull out a Warm Fuzzy. Warm Fuzzies were very much in demand because whenever somebody was given a Warm Fuzzy it made him feel warm and fuzzy all over. People who didn't get Warm Fuzzies regularly were in danger of developing a sickness in their back which caused them to shrivel up and die.

In those days it was very easy to get Warm Fuzzies. Any time that somebody felt like it, he might walk up to you and say, "I'd like to have a Warm Fuzzy." You would then reach into your bag and pull out a Fuzzy the size of a little girl's hand. As soon as the Fuzzy saw the light of day it would smile and blossom into a large. shaggy Warm Fuzzy. You then would lay it on the person's shoulder or head or lap and it would snuggle up and melt right against their skin and make them feel good all over. People were always asking each other for Warm Fuzzies, and since they were always given freely, getting enough of them was never a problem. There were always plenty to go around and as a consequence everyone was happy and felt warm and fuzzy most of the time.

One day a bad witch became angry because everyone was so happy and no one was buying her potions and salves. This witch was very clever and she devised a very wicked plan. One beautiful morning she crept up to Tim while Maggie was playing with their daughter and whispered in his ear, "See here, Tim, look at all the Fuzzies that Maggie is giving to Lucy. You know, if she keeps it up, eventually she is going to run out and then there won't be any left for you."

Tim was astonished. He turned to the witch and said, "Do you mean to tell me that there isn't a Warm Fuzzy in our bag every time we reach into it?"

And the witch said, "No, absolutely not, and once you run out, that's it. You don't have any more." With this, she flew away on her broom, laughing and cackling hysterically.

Tim took this to heart and began to notice every time Maggie gave up a Warm Fuzzy to someone else. Eventually he got very worried and upset because he liked Maggie's Warm Fuzzies very much and did not want to give them up. He certainly did not think it was right for Maggie to be spending all her Warm Fuzzies on the children and on other people. He began to complain every time he saw Maggie giving a Warm Fuzzy to somebody else, and because Maggie liked him very much, she stopped giving Warm Fuzzies to other people as often, and reserved them for him.

The children watched this and soon began to get the idea that it was wrong to give up Warm Fuzzies any time you were asked or felt like it. They, too, became very careful. They would watch their parents closely and whenever they felt that one of their parents was giving too many Fuzzies to others, they also began to object. They began to feel worried whenever they gave away too many Warm Fuzzies. Even though they found a Warm Fuzzy every time they reached into their bag, they reached in less and less and became more and more stingy. Soon people began to notice the lack of Warm Fuzzies, and they began to feel less and less fuzzy. They began to shrivel up and occasionally, people would die from lack of Warm Fuzzies. More and more people went to the witch to buy her potions and salves even though they didn't seem to work.

Well, the situation was getting very serious indeed. The bad witch, who had been watching all of this, didn't really want the people to die, so she devised a new plan. She gave everyone a bag that was very similar to the Fuzzy Bag except that this one was cold while the Fuzzy Bag was warm. Inside of the witch's bag were Cold Pricklies. Cold Pricklies did not make people feel warm and fuzzy, but made them feel cold and prickly instead. But, they did prevent people's backs from shriveling up. So, from then on, every time somebody said, "I want a Warm Fuzzy," people who were worried about depleting their supply would say, "I can't give you a Warm Fuzzy, but would you like a Cold Prickly?" Sometimes, two people would walk up to each other, thinking they could get a Warm Fuzzy, but one or the other of them would change his mind and they would wind up giving each other Cold Pricklies. So, the end result was that while very few people were dying, a lot of people were still unhappy and feeling very cold and prickly.

The situation got very complicated because, since the coming of the witch, there were less and less Warm Fuzzies around, so Warm Fuzzies, which used to be thought of as free as air, became extremely valuable. This caused people to do all sorts of things in order to obtain them. Before the witch had appeared, people used to gather in groups of three or four or five, never caring too much who was giving Warm Fuzzies to whom. After the coming of the witch, people began to pair off and to reserve all their Warm Fuzzies for each other exclusively. If ever one of the two persons forgot himself and gave a Warm Fuzzy to someone else, he would immediately feel guilty about it because he knew his partner would probably resent the loss of a Warm Fuzzy. People who could not find a generous partner had to buy their Warm Fuzzies and had to work long hours to earn the money. Another thing which happened was that some people would take Cold Pricklies - which were limitless and freely available - coat them white and fuzzy and pass them on as Warm Fuzzies. These counterfeit Warm Fuzzies were really Plastic Fuzzies, and they caused additional difficulties. For instance, two people would get together and freely exchange Plastic Fuzzies, which presumably should make them feel good, but they came away feeling bad instead. Since they thought they had been exchanging Warm Fuzzies, people grew very confused about this, never realizing that their cold prickly feelings were really the result of the fact that they had been given a lot of Plastic Fuzzies.

So, the situation was very, very dismal and it all started because of the coming of the witch who made people believe that some day, when least expected, they might reach into their Warm Fuzzy Bag and find no more.

Not long ago a young woman with big hips, born under the sign of Aquarius, came to this unhappy land. She had not heard about the bad witch and was not worried about running out of Warm Fuzzies. She gave them out freely, even when not asked. They called her the Hip Woman and disapproved of her because she was giving the children the idea that they should not worry about running out of Warm Fuzzies. The children liked her very much because they felt good around her and they, too, began to give out Warm Fuzzies whenever they felt like it. The grown-ups became concerned and decided to pass a law to protect the children from depleting their supplies of Warm Fuzzies. The law made it a criminal offense to give out Warm Fuzzies in a reckless manner. The children, however, seemed not to care and in spite of the law, they continued to give each other Warm Fuzzies whenever they felt like it and always when asked. Because there were many, many children, almost as many as grown-ups, it began to look as if maybe they would have their way.

As of now it is hard to say what will happen. Will the grown-up forces of law and order stop the recklessness of the children? Are the grown-ups going to join with the Hip Woman and the children in taking a chance that there will always be as many Warm Fuzzies as needed? Will they remember the days their children are trying to bring back when Warm Fuzzies were abundant because people gave them away freely?

QUESTIONS FOR YOUR ADULT

1. What is the largest organ in our body?
2. Strokes are nice. Why do we *need* them?
3. Why do we spend 24 hours a day getting strokes?
4. What is a Warm Fuzzy? (Give an example.)
5. What is a Cold Prickly? (Give an example.)
6. Name the 7 ways of getting strokes. How do you get yours mostly?
7. What's a "little Professor"? How does yours behave? Is he or she a "wise guy"? Does he/she hook P-A-C? Is he/she creative, imaginative, intuitive? Do you play your hunches?
8. What's a Ritual, a Pastime, a Game, an Activity, Intimacy, Fun, Withdrawal?
9. What's a Racket? What are your Rackets?
10. What's a Script? Do you know anything about yours? Can you change it? How?

EXERCISES

1. Draw up a Subjective Stroke Scale and keep a record for one day (1 week) of how you get your strokes. Are you satisfied? If not what can you change?
2. Be a game detective. Listen for games on TV; when people are talking in groups; in a restaurant. Learn to recognize them by the opening phrases. But don't tell them. Just learn what they are and later you'll be able to avoid getting into them and save yourself lots of pain.
3. Recognize games you play. Practice getting out.
4. What are some script messages you got when you were little? What did your Mother or Dad always say to you? One little girl is told, "You're a regular Florence Nightingale" after she put a bandaid on her brother's cut. Another is told, "She's not much in math, but what a cook!" "He can't draw, but he's sure fast with a buck." "A Born salesman." What did they tell you? Talk about it. Are you scripted? Do you want to change your script for a life plan of your own? How can you do it?

IDEAS AND WORDS TO LEARN MORE ABOUT

1. Warm Fuzzy
2. Cold Prickly
3. Negative & positive strokes
4. Subjective Stroke Scale
5. Time structuring functions: Withdrawal, etc.
6. Racket
7. Script

Chapter V

BEING OK, FEELING OK

"I to myself am dearer than a friend." Shakespeare

The first time I heard the term "OK", I thought it was something that Dr. Thomas A. Harris had made up. I thought, "He doesn't really know what he is talking about." I thought, "OK means all right, all is well, or 'OK?' like in, 'Do you understand me?' " But that isn't what OK means in TA language. "OK" in TA means you have *worth* as a person. You are important simply *because you exist*; because you are here and alive. You have worth to other people. You are able to think and figure things out without playing crooked games. You can make it. *You are a winner.*

WHAT OK MEANS

You were born OK. Everyone is OK when they are born. And we feel OK because we exist, because we breathe, eat, and drink, give off wastes, and sleep. Other people care about us and give us lots of free strokes. Strokes which feel good Dr. Steiner has called "Warm Fuzzies." Strokes which feel bad he calls "Cold Pricklies." In my book, *TA for Tots*, I talked a lot about Warm Fuzzies and Cold Pricklies and how to ask for Warm Fuzzies when you want them. If you want to have some fun sometime, read *TA for Tots!* It will give you a simple, fun review of some of the things that we're just touching on here, and if you want your younger brother or sister to become less of a pain, read it to them. But, I guess this isn't the first time you've heard of TA, so I don't want to spend a lot of time on things that you know. In this book, we've got a few new things to say. If you are new to TA, you can catch up by doing some outside reading. If you want to, you can read about strokes, Warm Fuzzies, Cold Pricklies, Frozzes and Prinzes, etc., in some of the books that are listed at the end of the book.

So, according to Dr. Harris, who wrote *I'm OK, You're OK*, "OK" means you are able to think, are worthwhile and important. When you were little, they called you an infant or a baby. You were OK, and you felt OK. But then, because you weren't able to do all the things that people expected you to do, like eat, sleep, run, feed yourself, be quiet, etc., you began to get the idea that maybe you were "not OK." That you weren't worthwhile, important, or able to think. You may have been helped along with this by some of the things you were told about yourself, like, "You're a bad, nasty, dirty, stupid, dumb kid, and a clumsy ox (my Dad's favorite). You're too fat, too thin, you're just like your Uncle Zoop." You were told this because Mother and Dad hoped that you would improve; that you would begin to do

"You are important simply because you exist."

the things they thought were important for you and for them. Maybe they wanted you to learn more quickly so you would avoid being like "Uncle Zoop (the Stoop)," so they told you, "Don't be stupid like your Uncle Zoop. Do you want to grow up to be a bum like him?" My mother used to say, "You can work with your back or your head. Take your pick." (There's nothing wrong with either - as a matter of fact, backworkers are healthier than headworkers - they live longer, too.) Of course, in the good old USA, we believe in using our head more and our backs less.

EARLY DECISIONS

But, what your Mother and Father didn't know was that, when they were telling you, "You are stupid," you believed them. They were so important to you. You may have gotten into your first bind when they said, "Don't be stupid." You know! You love them, and you want to please them. You're not sure whether they mean, "Be stupid (do it dumb) and please me," or "Do something right that I want you to do and please me." At first, you try to please them. Later on, you may get the idea that there's "no way to please them" because you just aren't able to do what they ask (at that time). So, you make your first loser's decision which is, "I can't." My Grandmother used to say, "Can't never could." I think "can't" means "won't." So, if you "won't", that's your choice. Now, if you had only said, "I can't right now," you wouldn't have been a loser. But, you said, "I can't." Probably you added to the "I can't" and "I never will be able to, and I don't care." (Baloney.) "So, I give up. I'm not OK. I'm not able. I'm not important. They don't like me unless I can do it their way, and I can't." If you had said, "I can't now," it would have helped you, but you didn't say that. So you made a decision, way back, when you were small, "I can't, and I never will be able to (and that makes me a loser)."

Now, as soon as you said, "I'm not OK (I can't, and I never will be able to)," you also told yourself something else. That something else was, "I'm not OK, but they are." They meaning everybody else in your world. You were really in a terrible position because if "I'm not OK, people won't love me. They won't give me any strokes. And, if they don't give me any strokes, I'm going to get sick and die. My spine will shrivel up. I'm going to get marasmus. Ow!" Then despair and panic! "What'll I do? Help! I Know! I'll act as if I'm OK (even though I'm not)." So, you decided to fool people into giving you strokes that you felt you were not going to get because you weren't "OK".

GETTING INTO GAMES

Thus, to stay alive, you made a decision: "I'm not OK; other people are OK." This provides the basis for most of the games that people play, described by Dr. Eric Berne in his book Games People Play, and by Dr. Claude Steiner, Dr. Harris and Dr. Muriel James in their books; and some of the games that I talked about in TA for Kids which, hopefully, you have read by now. But, just as an example of the kind of thing I'm talking about, a game is a crooked or hidden way of getting strokes from other people by fooling them. According to C. Steiner "A game is a recurring series of

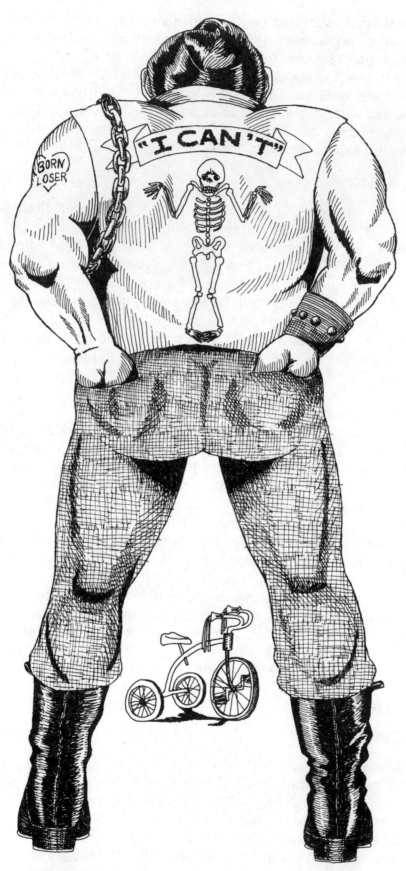

You made a decision when you were very small "I can't,
and I never will be able to and that makes me a loser."

ulterior (hidden) transactions, with a beginning (hook) middle (gimmick) and end and a pay-off (reward)''. You may feel you're a loser so you have to fool them because you believe "Not OK" people like you don't get strokes. Suppose, for instance, you are late coming home from school. You know when you get home, Mother's going to be upset. So, when she asks why you're so late, you say, "The reason I'm late from school is *because the teacher* kept me in. She didn't let me out on time, so I'm late." This is true. She did keep you in, and you can say, "If it wasn't for her, I would have been home on time." But, what is the real truth? The truth is, that if you had done your work and behaved yourself in school, according to the rules, you wouldn't have been kept in. Was it her fault or yours? Talk about that, right now. If you admit it's your fault, you figure you won't get any strokes. You'll probably get a lot of Cold Pricklies. So, you say, "If it wasn't for that dumb old teacher keeping me in, I'd have been home right on time, Mom." ("So please feel sorry for me for having been kept in, and *give that teacher* a hard time.") You see what I mean? *"If it wasn't for her, I'd be OK."* That's a game called *If It Wasn't For Her.* All of us play a lot of games in order to get good strokes or to avoid bad strokes. Some of them are *Mine's Better Than Yours, I'll Get Back At You, Now I'm Going To Get You, Look What You Did To Me, Look What You Got Me Into, What'll I Do?, Why Don't You-Yes But . . .* , and so on. Do you play any of them? If you want to know more about games played in school, read Ken Ernst's book *Games Students Play and What To Do About Them.* Mr. Ernst is a great guy. He teaches school and I'm told his students think he's OK. His book is about you and your teachers. It will help you get along better with game playing teachers, brothers and sisters, classmates and team mates.

LIFE POSITIONS

Now, let's get back to OKness. The first position that people take when they're born is, "I'm OK and everybody else is OK," or "I'm OK, You're OK." This is the life health position. You are a Prinz, and so is everyone else. You can be open, friendly, intimate, and safe. It's like being at home with everyone. Home is a place where you are safe, loved, protected, warm, OK. That's what makes us love home and folks. When home is not like that, people often look forward to leaving it as soon as legal.

When we get the feeling "I'm Not OK, You Are OK", we have decided that we're really not adequate, worthwhile, and important, but that everyone else is. So, if "I'm going to get any strokes, I'm going to have to fool them."

Some hopeless people decide "No matter what I do (play games or not), I'll never get any strokes and everyone else is a loser, too!" That's a pretty awful feeling because they are saying to themselves, "I'm not OK, and you're not OK," meaning *nobody* is OK. That's a pretty miserable world to be in, and they're very unhappy. They don't know, what to do about it.

There is one more life position which is pretty important for you to know about if you want to change from being a loser to a winner. This one is, "I'm OK, You're Not OK." As we have said before, some people, early in life, get the feeling that they are *not* OK, and that everyone else is OK.

"The first position that people take when they're born is "I'm OK, You're OK.""

From this position, they decide to be very, very good and to do what grown-ups want them to do so that they will get strokes. Thus, they become very *adaptive* and do whatever they are told. Sometimes, they find out that *no matter* what they do, they can't seem to please their important elders. I think that you may have felt that way a time or two. I know I have. But, if over and over the *PICs** are giving them a hard time (for instance, beating them up without any cause, punishing them because they're out of sorts themselves, treating them brutally by starving them, burning them, beating them, or deserting them) these youngsters get the feeling that the *PICs* around them are not very dependable, to say the least, and that all PICs and all other people are truly not OK; that since mothers and fathers, and those that they depend on are not OK, then no PIC is OK or to be trusted, EVER! These kids then decide to survive on their own; not to trust anyone older or in authority because they usually "rip you off," "cheat" you, if you depend on them. (Remember, "You can't trust anyone over 30."?) These brutalized or deprived youngsters decide to be against authority because "You can't trust anyone (especially if they're nice to you; that's just a way to fool you again)."

THE OK CORRAL

Why is this important to you? How can you change from a Not OK position, a loser's life plan, to an OK position? Well! Franklin Ernst, M.D. (he's Ken's older brother and a friend of Dr. Berne's) has pointed out that each of us uses all four positions. (Remember, *I'm OK - You're OK, I'm Not - You Are, I am - You're Not, and I'm Not - You're Not.*] Part of the time we feel, "I'm OK - You're OK." Sometimes, "I'm Not OK - Everyone else is OK." Sometimes, "I'm OK - But everyone else stinks." Sometimes, "Nobody is OK (I'm not OK - You're not OK)." He calls these four positions the "OK Corral." Here's what the OK Corral looks like:

"OK CORRAL"

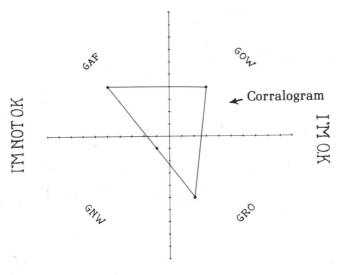

*People-in-Charge (who PIC on us).

He suggests that to know what your are like, draw your own "corral-ogram." What's a corralogram? Well, look! You know what a graph is. The upright line is called the ordinate; the horizontal line the abscissa. Now, if you make crossed lines (Fig. 1), you have four graphs. Measure in each direction how OK and Not OK you are. Find a point and connect up the lines. There's your corralogram. Watch.

Pt. 1 Suppose *I'm not OK* 5 points and 4 points *you are OK.*
Pt. 2 Suppose *I'm OK* 3 points and 4 points *you are OK.*
Pt. 3 Suppose *I'm OK* 2 points and 5 points *you're not OK.*
Pt. 4 Suppose *I'm not OK* 1 point and 1 point *you're not OK.*

How does this person feel most of the time? See, most of the time, I'm Not OK, and you (everyone else) are OK. Do I want that? No! I don't! I want to be a winner. Guess I'll have to change. But how? Here are some clues. George H. Weldon filled in the blocks with some ways winners and losers feel and behave. Maybe they'll help you change. Here they are:

LIFE POSITIONS

I'M OK, YOU'RE NOT OK

I'LL SHOW THEM WHO'S A WINNER
POWER MAKES ME FEEL BETTER
I DON'T TRUST ANYBODY
I GOTTA STAY ONE-UP ON EVERYBODY
I HURT OTHERS BEFORE THEY HURT ME
I'LL DRIVE AWAY ANYONE WHO GETS CLOSE
SOMEBODY WILL GET ME IN THE END
I'LL GET RID OF THEM (IT, ME) (GRO)

I'M NOT OK, YOU'RE OK

I'M A LOSER AMONG WINNERS
I FEEL BAD ABOUT MYSELF
I'M ANXIOUS AROUND OTHERS
I ALWAYS PUT MYSELF DOWN
I DO THINGS TO HURT MYSELF
I'LL KEEP MY DISTANCE
LIFE GOES ON AROUND ME
I'LL GET AWAY FROM THEM (GAF)

1 | 2
3 | 4

I'M NOT OK, YOU'RE NOT OK

SOME ARE BIGGER LOSERS THAN OTHERS
I FEEL BAD ABOUT MYSELF
I'M HOSTILE TOWARDS OTHERS
I PUT EVERYBODY DOWN
I SEEM TO HURT EVERYBODY
I'LL FIGHT OFF ALL INVADERS
I SEEM TO GET NOWHERE (GNW)

I'M OK, YOU'RE OK

WE'RE ALL MEANT TO BE WINNERS
I FEEL GOOD ABOUT MYSELF
I FEEL GOOD ABOUT OTHERS
I DON'T NEED TO PUT OTHERS DOWN
I DON'T WANT TO HURT ANYBODY
I'VE GOT NO WALLS TO PROTECT
LET'S GET ON WITH LIFE (GOW)

Notice the GRO, GAF, GOW and GNW? Wonder what that is? Well, Dr. Ernst says there are four ways to deal with life puzzles or problems. You can "Get Away From" (GAF), "Get Rid Of" (GRO), "Get Nowhere" (GNW), or "Get On With" (GOW) solving it. Only the last is in the winner's circle. Where do you want to be? Takes lots of guts and brains to make it. You have enough of both, just start using them — *right now!* Believe it! You can do it! How do I know? Because *you're OK!* Any other answer is your two-year-old Child talking. Are you going to let that little kid run your life? Or, some kindly but mistaken PIC who told you, "You're not OK." Real independence comes when *you* (Adult) decide to be a winner. Will you? Now? Good! I'm with you.

QUESTIONS FOR YOUR ADULT

1. Is being OK and feeling OK, the same thing? How do they differ? Can you feel not OK and still be OK? How come? Discuss this.
2. Is it possible that brother or sister annoys you but are still OK? How can you let them know that? Why should you?
3. What is a game? What games do you play? How do you feel about the games that go on at your house?
4. What is a life position? How do we get it? What is yours? Do you want to change it? How will you go about it?
5. George Weldon drew an OK Corral and filled in some typical things which people do, think, and feel when they are in one of the life positions. Can you add to them? List from your own experience or observations of others.

EXERCISES

1. Ask someone for Warm Fuzzies.
2. Look up Ken Ernst's book. ('Games Students Play, and What To Do About Them.]
3. Draw your OK Corralogram. See if you want to keep it that way. How will you change it?
4. Send me a list from 5 above. I'd really like to have it.
5. Describe a game you play or have observed. Define the hook, the gimmick, the end, and the pay off. Example: What should I do? is a hook - Well, why don't you . . . ? Yes but (repeated) is the gimmick Silence is end of game. What do you think is the payoff?

IDEAS AND WORDS TO LEARN MORE ABOUT

1. Life positions
2. TA Games
3. OK Corral
4. GRO, GAF, GNO, GNW

Chapter VI

HONESTY, TRUST, AND FREEDOM

*"Your first contract was, and your last contract will be,
a trade-off of your responsibility for your freedom."*
                                                    Al Freed

"Be in by eleven, dear." (Discount)* "Oh! Mother, do I have to come in at 11:00? We want to go out and get something to eat afterwards. The dance isn't over until 11:00." "I know, dear, but *I* don't like you running around till all hours. You never know what's going to happen" (Discount).

"You can hear the hidden talk that's going on underneath."

*Discounting occurs when you or someone else acts as if you or your feelings don't count, are not real, not important. ("I'm no good" is a self-discount). Nobody can do that (discount the possibility of solving the problem). You can discount or lessen your own "problem" - dilemma, or feeling (too big, too small) by denial ("This isn't true"). Finally, you can discount facts (the real world) by denying or negating what others know is truth based on hard evidence. For example, "You didn't tell me" (when others heard you being told), "I never said I would" (when others heard you). "He didn't say it to me, so I don't know it." Behind every game and racket is a discount. Behind every passive behavior is a discount." See *Growing, Growing,* by MacDonald Hawley, 1973.

"Mother! Nothing's going to happen. (Discount) We're just going to go to Hamburger Haven for a snack. Then we'll be right home. We're not going to *do* anything." I guess you can hear the second conversation (hidden talk) that's going on underneath the first one, where Mother is saying, "I don't want you to mess around and get pregnant after the dance," and you're telling her that you have no intentions of making out, getting pregnant, or getting busted. That's what you're both thinking (hidden talk) but, of course, because you've been taught very carefully for a long time not to talk about things that personal, neither of you feel free to talk about it. Well, maybe that's OK; maybe it isn't. I don't know. You and I can't change the history of what's been going on between mothers and daughters for a long time. The way Mother was raised, she doesn't feel comfortable talking about it, and the way you've been raised, you don't feel comfortable talking to Mother about it. You may talk to everybody else, but not to Mother or Dad.

Maybe we can talk about something else: that is, at what point can Mother feel good about your going out? When can she feel confident that you know enough to protect yourself? At what point can you feel that Mother trusts you, and you can trust yourself? How long will it be before you are strong enough and wise enough to take on the total responsibility for your own behavior? When will you be able to level with Mother about her feeling "just awful" about what you are doing?

THE OLD AND THE NEW — WHAT'S FOR YOU?

You probably also want to know how can you talk to Mother so that she knows her feelings count with you, even if you don't agree with her ideas? You're going to need a thorough understanding of yourself and your folks, because everybody wants to be completely "free" and to feel that he or she counts. You want to be independent; want to "do your own thing." You don't want anybody to tell you what to do. You resent, like mad, somebody taking for granted that you're going to get into trouble, that you don't have good sense, good morals, good values, or good self-control. You resent that Mother feels you have to be supervised (spied on) much like youngsters did when Mother and Grandmother were growing up. They used to have chaperones to make sure that, "in their innocence," they did nothing that elders wouldn't approve of. Well, we've come a long way from then, but the dilemmas are still the same. How we're handling them is different. If you're going to take on the total responsibility for yourself, you know, do the job yourself; if you're going to discard all the "old-fashioned ideas" about values and morality, then you're going to need some kind of new ones for you. You're going to have to have some kind of rules by which you run your life. You don't have to use the old ones! You don't have to use Grandmother's! They didn't work too well even for her — as anyone can tell you. But, you're going to have to have *some* values and rules for behavior. Otherwise, you may get confused. You won't know how to make rapid decisions that are needed to protect yourself at times when your Kid is running things. Know what I mean? You want to do or have something (from pot to sex) which could be harmful to you. What rule do you follow? Does anything go?

THE FIRST CONTRACT

All this goes back in your history a little bit. You know, when you were small, a little infant in a crib, and you didn't have to take care of yourself. Mother and Dad did that, and maybe Grandmother or whoever was around (babysitters, big sister, big brother, whatever). But, they took care of you. Some better, some worse. But, at least they fed you, or you wouldn't be here, and they probably picked you up and gave you some strokes, a bath, things like that. Anyhow, they did enough to keep you alive, you see, so they "took care of you." Maybe not the way you liked it, but they did. At that

"You didn't have any freedom; you were completely dependent."

time, you didn't have any responsibility for taking care of yourself, and *you didn't have any freedom; you didn't have any independence.* You were completely dependent, and that was OK with you because then you didn't have any way of becoming free. But, a year or so passed and you began to look around and found that there were some great things to do if people would let you. Like, it would be nice to be able to roam around the playpen. That it was kind of fun to stand up, sit down, pull yourself up, have toys, and so on. And Mother then became a little bit freer with you. She let you do more things. Right then, she gave you a taste of independence - and responsibility. When she let you roam around the play-pen, she made a contract with you. She would go out of the room and say, "My baby's going to be all right. She can take care of herself like a big girl (boy)." That was the agreement. It was like she had said, "I'll leave you alone, honey, if you take care of yourself." And as if you said to Mother (if you could have spoken), "Oh, Mommy, I'm going to be just fine. You can trust me." Right then, there was born a mutual trust — *a contract.* Mother was to come back and see if you needed her, but meanwhile, you would be OK, take care of yourself, be safe, and have fun. You felt good about that, and she felt that she could trust you to take care of yourself (in the playpen) and not to climb out, not to throw things out, not get your arm twisted, and so on. A whole lot of things went into that first contract — a trade-off of responsibility for freedom. She would look in on you occasionally so that you would feel safe and she would feel OK about it. Well, that was great; that was a good contract, and it worked out.

YOU GREW AND THE CONTRACTS DID, TOO.

Later on, when you got a little bigger, you began to walk around pretty well. You were then allowed to go out in the yard and sit or play in the grass. Maybe the back yard, maybe the front yard, but wherever it was, there was that same contract. "You take care of yourself and I want you to have fun and be safe. When you need something, you just call me and I'll come. If you get into trouble in anyway, you just let me know and I'll get you out of it. Okay?" And you were telling Mother, in effect, "Hey! I'm getting to be a big kid now. I can take care of me. You just go ahead, Mother, and do your work and if I want you, I'll call you, but let me have some fun by myself. I'm OK. I'm safe. You can trust me not to leave the yard and not to get into too much difficulty." So, that was the contract.

Next time, it was out playing on the sidewalk with youngsters your own age. Later on, it was authority to get on the bus by yourself and go to school (and to come home right away). Still later, it was to go out and play and come in at a certain time, and so on. And each time you gained something, as did Mother. You gained some freedom and safety. Freedom from each other for longer and longer periods of time with more and more need for you to use your head to take care of yourself. Less and less need for her to know exactly where you were and what you were doing every minute like she did when you were an infant. Well, OK, that works out fine just so long as you keep yourself safe in a way that makes sense to her and to other people around you. This is the beginning of the responsibility/freedom graph.

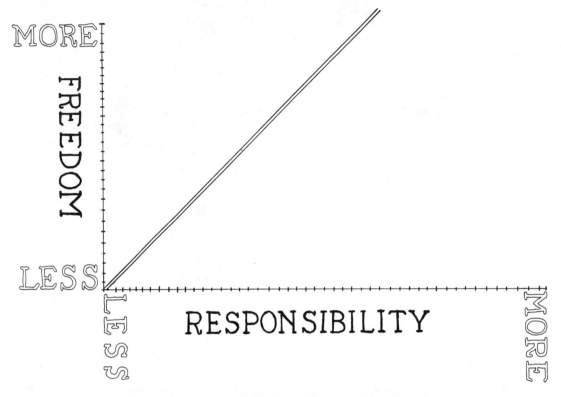

Responsibility/Freedom Graph

YOU CAN'T DO JUST ANYTHING YOU WANT

When you are out playing, there are other people playing. When you are in school, there are other people in school, and they, too, have needs. So, this is where we are at this point. You're about to take on a bigger chunk of freedom. Like going out on dates and coming in on time. Are you beginning to break those contracts you made a long time ago? If so, Mother and Dad get very scared, for you and for them. They've invested a large share of their lives in your becoming a person of worth. You see, Moms and Dads often feel Not OK, too. And they place great hope on you to make it so that their lives will have been worthwhile. In this way, Moms and Dads live through their children.

You may not know or care about Mother and Dad's hopes at this point. Maybe you feel that's too heavy a load. Maybe you feel you've let them down. You may then begin to think of yourself as no good, a failure, that nobody could love you, *you feel like a "froz."* So, because you want and need strokes, you begin to try to get them from your "friends", and when one Very Special Friend (VSF) gives them to you, you feel great. You're ready to trade everybody else in — Mother, Dad, brother, sister, teacher, principal, cops — for those great strokes from that VSF. Trouble is, you also may turn in your new found freedom and independence. Because, as you may have found, boyfriends and girlfriends are sometimes more

75

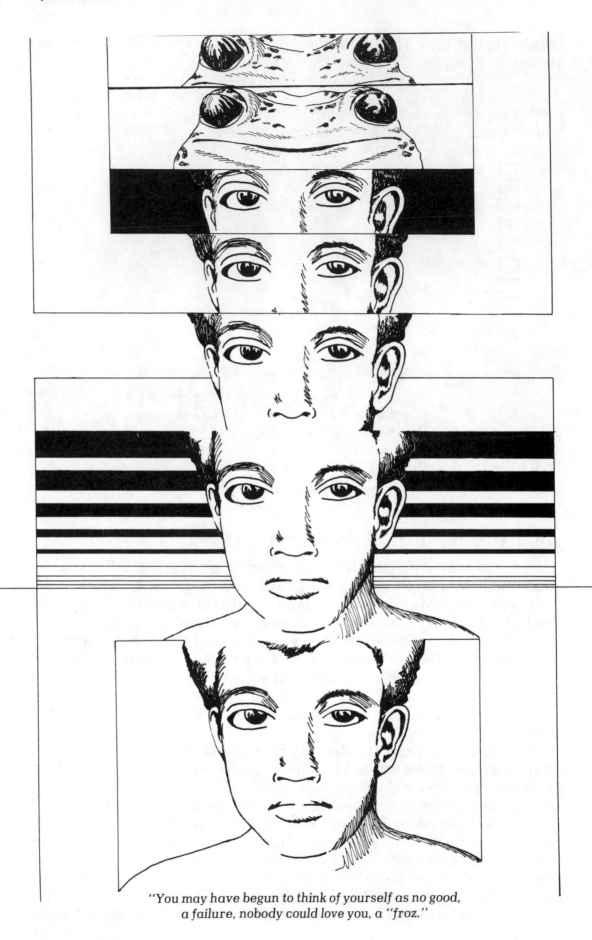

"You may have begun to think of yourself as no good,
a failure, nobody could love you, a "froz."

restricting than your folks. Ever go steady? You can't go out with any other person; can't have other friends; can't go out if VSF is away (unless you break the contract and feel guilty; get caught and feel embarrassed) and so on. No way to find out who you are or who he is. Why do you feel attracted? Why a VSF and not someone else? *Do you know on what basis you selected your friend?* Was it your Parent and his Child? Your Child and his Child (he's fun!)? Children don't like contracts and hate to keep them. They have fun. Okay if it's temporary, but suppose you have to take on the whole ball of wax — rent, laundry, cooking, cleaning, insurance, traffic tickets, clothes, babies, etc., etc. You'll need more than a C-C relationship to make it.

"You'll need more than a Child to Child relationship to make it."

YOUR VALUE SYSTEM

Teen years are a wonderful time for shaping up your value system. What do you (not Mother or Father) believe is OK for you? Check it out with others — maybe in a TA group because there you can get straight feedback, or with others you know and trust. I don't trust rap-groups because they are often inexpertly led by people who profess great depth of knowledge and wisdom, but who are often speaking with authority from their angry and rebellious Child and making generalizations based on their limited experience. They are sometimes one-sided — "us against the world." In a TA group, you can figure out what's right for you for yourself without a put-down, and you can change your mind, too. That's important.

The second idea here is, "How do I let Mother know her worries are important to me even though her ideas don't jibe with mine?" Back to Dr. Pemberton — remember the 4, 5, 6 idea? (4) "Mom, you want me in by 11:00, right?" (Getting data.) (5) To yourself, "I don't like that at all — spoils my fun. No chance to make out or anything." (6a) To yourself, "Guess Mom's afraid if I stay out too late that I'll get turned on and go all the way with Tom." (6b) Say to Mom, in your own words, "Mom, you're afraid if I stay out too late, your 'Little Red Riding Hood', namely me, will get ripped off by that big bad wolf, namely Tom." (You're being straight now, so she can be straight with you.) Also, you've told her you know about her feelings of fear and love for you and you care about her. Now she can be straight with you and herself. Mother (5) to herself, "Ah!" She knows! Yes, I am worried about that. But maybe she can handle that herself OK." Mother (6a) to herself, "She's not afraid, and feels she can handle being out late." Mother (6b) to you. "You're not too worried about handling your feelings and Tom's when you get close. You'd rather I trusted you and would not put my worries on you. I'll work on that, because I do worry, but I think you're OK. By the way, is there anything you'd like to know that I can help you with?"

Do you think this a more productive conversation than the one at the beginning of this Chapter? Do you think you can make it work for you?

QUESTIONS FOR YOUR ADULT

1. What is a discount? Do you discount yourself? Others? How do you do that?
2. What is passive behavior? What's wrong with being passive?
3. What are your moral values? Your morals? Are they yours or someone else's?
4. What is a contract? Why are they important?
5. Talk about responsibility and freedom: what is your main gripe about this at home? In school?
6. Discuss, "Child in us hates contracts." Why is this important?

EXERCISES

1. Tell how you used a 4-5-6 this week to be more effective in transacting with someone.
2. Give an example of someone else or yourself in a crisis talk. Tell how this could have changed.
3. Act out a situation where there is a "hidden" conversation. Two of you have the real conversation while two others report on the hidden ideas.

WORDS AND IDEAS TO LEARN MORE ABOUT

1. Discount
2. Contract
3. Value system
4. Values
5. VSF (Very Special Friend)

Chapter VII

STRAIGHT AND CROOKED TALK:
APOLOGIES AND GAMES

> *"Games are good or bad as to their nature —*
> *all may be perverted."*   Dr. Johnson

Most of us, at some time or other, do things that cross transactions with others. This may lead to hurt or angry feelings and to "manufacturing Brown Stamps" (*TA for Kids*). When we cross a transaction, usually it is for our own benefit. When we get angry, it is because we feel like getting

"Most of us, at some time or other, do things that cross a transaction from someone else."

angry. (I have a right (P) to be angry (C).) If we tell somebody off, we get a feeling of satisfaction out of that. If we take something that belongs to someone else, or if we spill something that messes up somebody else's place, we are not being too concerned about their comfort, but our own.

MISTAKES AND OK PEOPLE

OK People make mistakes once. Not OK People repeat their errors and apologize repeatedly. Even an accident is often due to failure to take the time to think about what I'm doing. When someone called an error to my attention, I would usually say, "I'm sorry." Then I wanted immediate forgiveness (strokes) for the goof. "Well? I said I was *sorry.*" ("What else do you want?") In this way, I won two ways. First by the luxury of not being careful. That's one "plus" that I got out of it. I may even have gotten some excitement and fun in doing things that offended other people. (Remember, Cold Pricklies are better than *no* strokes.) Then, I added insult to injury and tried to get the offended person to forgive me and get some more strokes. If they didn't, I would get angry again and say, "Well! I *said* I was *sorry!*" (As if that changed everything.) If I say, "Oh, please forgive me. I'm terribly sorry. Can you ever forgive me?," and the other person says, reluctantly, "Well . . . yes, that's all right. Let's forget it." "It" means that he got hurt while you had "fun" and then got off free.

PHONY STROKES

Apologies are phony ways of getting strokes. Instead of apologies, I'll accept a "no repeat" contract. Thus, whenever anyone comes late to an appointment with me, and they say, "I'm sorry!", I say, "Look, you're OK with me to be late, but please don't say you're sorry. I don't like your being late, so please *don't do it again.*" That's the basis for a better contract. In other words, "I like you but I don't like your being late" is much straighter than the "I'm sorry, Oh that's OK" bit. In this way, I won't reward you for having hurt, insulted, or inconvenienced me. I ask that you enter into an agreement with me not to do it again because it wasn't pleasant. I also avoid giving apologies. If I have offended someone, I might say, "I goofed and I won't do that again." I don't explain and I don't defend. The person may feel a little better if I admitted that I made a mistake and agree not to do it again.

My parents don't love me. They make me come home at eleven every night!

My parents don't love me. They don't care how late I stay out at night!

My parents don't love me. They're always going somewhere without me!

My parents don't love me. They never leave me alone!

"One way of getting stro

82

"OK PEOPLE AVOID GAMES"

OK People make mistakes, but they make the effort not to make them more than once. And they say it clearly. They don't blame other people and say, "Well! If it wasn't for you, this wouldn't have happened." They recognize that they goofed and they attempt to correct that kind of behavior in the future. We mentioned earlier about games. Games are hidden ways of getting strokes. People who play TA games are not aware of playing. That's one sign of a game. They usually come up with very plausible reasons for their actions. Games always happen more than once. So, if you find the same thing happening a number of times, begin to suspect a game and try to find out what you're getting out of it or avoiding (blame, etc.). The Pay-off of a game often helps you to understand your need and to change your behavior.

IT'S BETTER THAN NOTHING, OR IS IT?

One way of getting strokes is to get yourself kicked (Cold Pricklies). Frequently, boys and girls say they think that their folks don't care about them — for one reason or another. For example, if her mother didn't tell her when to come in at night, I've heard a girl say, "Well, she doesn't care about me. She doesn't care if I stay out all night or not." If her folks are

...to get yourself kicked."

strict, the same youngster might say, "They don't care how I feel." So, the behavior of the mothers or fathers can be interpreted in a number of different ways. Another person told me, "My mother didn't care about me. All she cared about was making money." That person's mother was working her fingers and soul to the bone to try to keep clothing on the children, and to get them food and shelter. She spent 18 or 19 hours a day working and had no time or energy to give them much needed strokes. The youngsters interpreted that as, "Mother doesn't care; doesn't love us." When you are young, your Kid is the one making the decisions and your Kid doesn't really figure things out. Your Kid only feels. So, if Mother or Dad aren't there, it becomes easy for the Kid to say, "They don't love me, or they would come home and take care of me, and they wouldn't turn me over, to a dumb old babysitter. So, I guess Mother (or Daddy) doesn't love me."

Sometimes you can't get the kind of strokes you like — Warm Fuzzies. Then, you may think the best bet is to get Cold Pricklies. So, we find some kids playing some pretty hard Kick Me games in order to get strokes. If you frequently make contracts and don't keep them and then get punished, maybe it's time to take a look. Say, "Hey, this is a pretty dumb way I have of getting strokes. Maybe I would be better off if I began to get out of the game and act in a way that I am sure will help me to win (and I can win because I'm a winner), where I can get positive strokes or Warm Fuzzies."

THE SCHOOL GAME

I'm sure you've seen people in school who deliberately aggravate the teacher; deliberately get booted out of class or expelled from school. And you wonder about them. "Why do they do that? They don't have to do that," you say. They are pretty good guys. But maybe they're not very good students. They may have difficulty learning. They've found out that they can't get A's or B's or C's, so they figure out how to get prickly strokes because they can't get Warm Fuzzies. The way to get them is to do something to hook the teacher. A recent study by D.R.G. Erskine[16] seems to show that kids in the worst trouble at school (truant, absent, late, failing, referred as high as 50 times) changed markedly for the better when they learned about P,A,C and themselves. Then they know who they were, where they were coming on from (P,A, or C) and how to get what they needed. Their grades improved, their lateness and absence decreased, and they were in trouble in school and out far, far less.

COPS AND ROBBERS

Another way that kids have of getting strokes when they feel they can't get them at home or school, is to get into a game of "Cops and Robbers." Remember when you were young you used to play "Hide and Go Seek?" The fun in Hide and Go Seek is in getting caught. When you get spotted, everybody runs shrieking and tries to get "Home" or "in clear" before the "it" person does. Well, "Cops and Robbers" is a later years TA variety of that. The way to get strokes out of "Cops and Robbers" is to do something against the rules at school or against the law and then make sure you get caught. It's not as much fun to get away with it because then nobody knows that *you* did it. You don't get any strokes. But, if you get caught, there's excitement and a *need* to be rescued (loved), and that's stroking. There is also the fun of competing with the People In Charge (PIC); trying to best them, trying to put them down, or to "get back at them." Sometimes, to fool them, you plot with somebody else about how you are going to get back at PIC's like teachers, principals, parole officers, or psychologists. Thus, the way to get strokes in "Cops and Robbers" is to act in a way that is cool, but which is intended to get you some negative strokes. You can't lose, really. If

*"The way to get strokes in "Cops and Robbers"
is to act cool to get some negative strokes."*

you "win" (Pull it off), you get some positive strokes from your partners. If you "lose" (get busted), you get kicked and you play "If it weren't for them," or "It's all their (cops, judges) fault." Perhaps even get expelled (Wow!) from school. Then it's the stuck-up kids, that teacher, the principal, the stupid psychologist who are at fault. You also "get back" at Mother and Dad and make them feel bad. Maybe you get "forgiven" by your PIC (Mother and Dad, Principal, Counselor), which is the pay-off your unconscious Kid is going for. That's your real pay-off. Being forgiven in spite of everything. You can be sure that if you are into the same thing over and over, there is a game going on. You may be going for strokes that you don't feel you can get by acting in a more responsible way. The first step in getting out of a game is to recognize you're in one. To learn more about that, read Muriel James' book called *People*,[17] or Ken Ernst's book *Games Students Play*.[12] Learn how to avoid games and win.

"The first step in getting out of a game is to recognize you're in one."

FRIENDS AND LOVERS

TA is pretty important in all of your relationships, but none probably more so than the kind that you have with other people your age, whether of the same or opposite sex. Unhappiness occurs when you don't understand where you are coming from (P,A, or C) and you don't understand where your friend is in his or her thinking. If you are going to be more effective with people, if you are going to be more comfortable with them, if you are going to achieve more lasting friendships, and especially a longer lasting, intimate or loving relationship, you must understand your own feelings, your own values, beliefs and goals in living. Only then will you understand people who are important to you.

Here are some examples. You've often heard people say that they would just "love to know" a special boy or girl, but are afraid to ask them for a date. They suffer all sorts of tortures and embarrassments. Ask their friends to "find out if he likes me" and things like that. It has always puzzled me why they didn't take a more direct route. When I ask, they say, "Oh! I wouldn't dare! I wouldn't be found dead doing that. You're not supposed to just go up to a girl or a guy and say, "Hey, I would like to know you better. How about my coming over to see you sometime?" I think, if you can't do that, you've got some not OK things to look at. There is nothing wrong with asking for a date. You're thinking, "Well, suppose she says no!" Then you've got your answer.

Of course, there are a lot of better ways to lead up to this which makes success more likely. What strokes her — a rose, a favorite book, help when she needs it, kind words, smiles and glad greetings, approval for what she (or he) does. In other words, being a friend. A friend is someone who likes you. And before a date, it's good to become a friend. The date will be more fun and probably turn out better. But the fear of being rejected is probably what is going on in you. Fear that someone might turn you down. Reject you. Just like grownups do. Here you are hoping she'll like YOU!

I always think of Peanuts and the "little red-headed girl." What a tragic story that is. Peanuts loves the little red-headed girl, but he never asks her to be his friend. Then she goes away and he never sees her again. I'm sure we've all had the little red-headed girls or boys in our lives. We always realize how foolish it was afterward, rather than coming out and saying, "Hey! I think it would be great to be friends with you." Usually, if you are going to be friends, and you like each other, the other person will be glad you asked. If not, what did you lose? One of the things that helps is to know where you are coming from when you talk to someone. Also, where they are. How can you do this? How can you know where the other person is? (P,A,C!)

HOW TO GET WHAT YOU WANT!

Boys traditionally are expected by girls to ask them for dates. Most boys are hesitant and unsure how to do this at first. Girls need to know how to help them do it because many boys find it scary to ask for a date or even for friendship with a girl. Of course, with the new values it's becoming more OK for girls to invite boys to things. But they have hesitancy, too. "What if he says no? I'd die!" Well, you won't, but maybe you'd like to.

"Most people are hesitant and unsure how to ask for a date."

87

Good strokes are never out of place, especially if they are in good taste. "Good strokes in good taste" is a good rule. For example, you don't go up and tell a girl that she has a great body. She probably already knows that. She probably is more interested in whether you are fun to be with than your "admiration" of her. If you admire her, you might tell her that she's pretty, that she looks like the kind of person you would like to know. Be specific. Admire a thing she or he wears (ring, etc.). Avoid criticism, even helpful ones. If you don't like the person as they are, find someone you do like.

Another way is to have some idea of what the person likes to do. Follow the what, where, when, and why rule. When asking for a date, say, "I have a couple of tickets (what) to the Music Circus (where) on Tuesday night (when) to see 'Annie Get Your Gun' (why), which is a great show. Would you like to go with me?" This will probably be more successful than, "Will you go out with me? (Giggle, giggle, blush)." If it's a dance, you might prepare for a date by saying, "There's a Junior Prom coming up and I know you are a good dancer. Can I come over tonight or would you like to come over tonight (when) and see if I dance (what) well enough (why) to make it fun for you? Do you think we could try dancing (how) and see if we enjoy

"The practice might be as much fun as the real thing."

it?'' See the what, where, when, why, and how? Something like that is usually OK and not too committing to either of you at first. If you don't know this young lady or young man, and even if you do, and you say, ''How about going to the Prom with me?,'' she or he doesn't know whether you are a stumblebum on a dance floor or a ''Fred Astaire'' with whom it would be fun. So, you have to recognize that the other person may not feel any more certain about themselves than you do! That they may want to get acquainted before they commit themselves to a ''big'' date. You'll feel better, too, if you feel OK about each other *before* you go out on a date. Probably the practice will be as much fun as the Prom. Be aware of what her or his folks are like, and what they like. You're not dating *them,* but they'll help you if you suit them. Just because you like their son or daughter doesn't mean they lose all rights to her or him. Remember, they saw her or him first and care very much about her or him.

MAKING NEW FRIENDS

Because you like someone, you want them to like you, doesn't mean that you have given them any reason to do so. Be aware of where you are coming from. Is it your Adult, or is it your Kid saying, ''I want, I want, I want.'' Are you figuring things out, or are you coming on from your Critical Parent, telling them what is wrong with them? Criticism turns people off. Sometimes, helping too much does, too. Are you coming on from your Nurturing Parent, protecting people, helping them, sacrificing for them, and then feeling ripped off? Giving people support in what they do is usually pleasant for them, and you can be more honest when you detect truthful and nice things to say, rather than to make things up simply to flatter them. But flattery is not all that bad. People like to get good strokes; to hear nice things even if they're not totally true. But, as Larry Mart says, ''Find 'hidden gold' in others and make them shine.'' Flattery is all right, and is never out of place. People *need* to be stroked, and there is never enough. (Read Claude Steiner's *Fuzzy Tale.*) If you're more comfortable, because your Parent Tape tells you always tell the truth, then find *nice things* to say about a person that are true. But, stay away from the negative. Get into the *positive stroking business* and you will find that dates are easier to get and more fun.

Girls tend to be less aggressive than boys because they've been taught to wait to be asked. Don't be a shrinking wall flower waiting to be picked. Go for what you want! But with finesse. Just as you wouldn't like being grabbed (not always), some boys — especially shy ones — feel very not OK about themselves (like you). So, telling them they're OK with you will help you both. I think you can disregard the old idea that boys must always ask girls for dates. Girls can invite boys to many things — parties, dances, to study, to a show, dutch treat game, a picnic, a swim, game of tennis, and so on. Make and keep it informal and unimportant. It's not the end of the world if he comes to see you or doesn't, or if it turns out to be a flop. I once knew someone who got the family to buy new furniture because she had a special date. He was unimpressed. How sad. Just be you. You're OK. And eventually you'll find someone just right for you. You will! Because you like yourself, others will, too. So, start liking you for your good points (find them) and improving what you don't like. Get help if you need it. But like yourself. You're OK!

QUESTIONS FOR YOUR ADULT

1. What is a brown stamp? How do we get them? What's a good thing to do with them? Why?
2. Why are apologies kind of gamey? What's a better thing to do than to give offense and then ask for forgiveness?
3. Do you know anyone who is forever saying, "I'm sorry." How do you feel about that? Them?
4. What can you do when you've goofed?
5. What is a friend? Do you have friends? How can you get more?

EXERCISES

1. Practice talking to an empty chair. Make believe it's the person you want to ask for a date. Try it a number of different ways until you feel comfortable. Get Dad or Mom to listen after you've gotten comfortable. Try it out on sister or brother.
2. Check yourself to see how many "I'm sorries" you're giving away each day. Try another way and be aware of the change in you and the other person.
3. In class, practice finding the "hidden gold" in five people. Write out your discoveries and then give them to each other (without signing your name.)

IDEAS AND WORDS TO LEARN MORE ABOUT

1. Brown stamps
2. Cops and Robbers
3. Apologies vs contracts
4. Hidden Gold

Chapter VIII

THE OLD AND THE NEW VALUES
(OR, DOING IT "MY WAY")

*"The wisdom of one generation will
be folly in the next."*   Priestley

Very often, when people come to my office, I find them puzzled about what to believe in. They say the new ways of living are in conflict with their religious teachings, or their most firmly held beliefs. "Stop and render assistance" conflicts with headlines of dire things which happen to "good samaritans" in the news. Sometimes your own feelings are in conflict with some of the things we know that we ought or ought not do (P). People frequently play a pastime called "In our society today" or as Eric Berne spelled it, "Inarsisiety," or "Nowadaze." These are related to another pastime called "Ain't It Awful." Do you hear people play these? Do you ever play "Wonder Why?"

Another example is when you want to lose weight. You know that you *should*, because *it's good for your health*. The doctor told you, "You shouldn't be so fat." "I hate being fat, but *I like to eat!*" (C).

I shouldn't eat so much! (P)

Being fat is not healthy. (A)

I like to eat !!! (C)

"There are different things going on."

So, there are usually two different things going on inside you. Of course, you and I know now that the inside conflict is going on between the Parent (which tells us what we should do), backed up by our Adult (which usually makes sense), and our Kid (which likes to eat). I know that if I'm too heavy, my body won't function too well. I won't look "nice," and won't have as much fun (not true). So, we should go on a diet. But the Kid says, "Yeah, but! Yeah, but! Yeah, but!" Someone called this internal argument "Stinking thinking."

YEARNINGS VS. LEARNINGS

There are many of us who feel guilty over our wants and yearnings and our learnings. We are torn between what we've learned as children from Mother and Dad, and our religious teachings, and what we are currently feeling in terms of new sensual strivings (horny, hot, sexy, etc.). Often we are afraid if we get angry or express our feelings, "if I ever 'let it out', I'll go crazy; not be able to stop; kill somebody," and so on.

A number of years ago, I wrote a paper called *My Parent the Robot, Or the Internal Dialogue.* I thought, at the time, that the internal dialogue (talk) was a TA game, but Dr. Claude Steiner assured me that this was merely internal talk between Ego (Self) States. A game, by Berne's definition, must take place between two or more people. One person speaking is a monologue. So, a TA game is a social thing, a dialogue or talk between 2 or more people. Internal talk, between our ego states, is something else.

BE FRIENDS WITH YOURSELF

A lot of internal dialogue or talk goes on between our Parent, our Adult, and our Child. I think this is great. It's healthy. It's important that you have these internal talks and when one is talking, the other two should really listen because in that way, you'll get acquainted with what's going on inside you. You know, it used to be said, "If you talk to yourself, you're crazy." I say *if you don't talk to yourself, you can go crazy.* So, it's very important that you talk to and listen to yourself. Your body knows.

Earlier, I said you can *be your own best friend* (YOBF). One way to be YOBF is to listen to yourself. Especially, listen to your body. Your body knows what it needs to stay healthy. Not always, but frequently, the things that we've learned are incorrect and impose uncomfortable limits on our body. For example, people were taught to keep their windows shut at night because night air was supposed to be bad for you. The air in the bedrooms was most unpleasant (yeuch).

THE BODY KNOWS

The body knows. *Will Schutz* tells that while visiting a town in the eastern U.S., he felt a cold coming on. He began to ask himself why he felt sick. What was it he didn't like about where he was? He realized he didn't like being in the East and in that town. He changed his plans and flew back home the next day and immediately his cold disappeared.

The body knows and acts to balance itself. When you are running and need more energy in your muscles, the lungs take in more air, and more oxygen goes into the blood stream until you feel better (get your "second wind"). Restricting our bodies with cultural rules often upsets us. "Don't show your feelings" leads to ulcers and high blood pressure. Always showing feelings makes for an unstable personality. So, you see, we must use our Adult in regulating our Kid and not necessarily obey all restrictions imposed on us by other people's rules and morals. These can and sometimes do make us sick. So, it's very important that you begin to listen to what your body is telling you. For example, the feelings that arise out of fear or out of unsatisfied drives (hunger, sex, fatigue) usually result in tension or uptight feelings. Many of us go unsatisfied so much of our lifetime that to stand it, we develop a heavy armor of tight connective muscle or fatty tissue. This restricts our movements so badly that we can't do what we'd like to do. We must begin to pay attention to our bodies and not condemn ourselves to living in a prison of our own making.

PLUG IN YOUR ADULT

Good sense (A) must take the place of "rules" if we are to discard rules of school, home, medicine, or religion, and that only comes with time and experience. So, take your time. Don't throw out old rules till you've had time to get some *Adult* facts. That takes study, reading, discussing and research. Remember, old rules have lasted because in general they worked to keep people safe and reasonably happy. Challenge them but don't disregard them until you have something better than "I like it" or "don't like it" to go on.

Now, immediately some of you who have had heavy religious training are going to say, "Well, we can't just let the body do whatever it wants. That's sinful to allow the body to express itself. We *must not have feelings* that we're *not supposed* to have." I can only tell you that *your body does have the feelings.* They are as much a part of you as your big toe. But what you

*"Repression leads to feelings of guilt simply because
we express our natural feelings."*

do with them becomes the dilemma. Some religious groups may teach that feelings are bad. This is in direct conflict with the natural functions of our bodies. Repression leads to great discomfort and expression results in terrible feelings of guilt, feelings of being not OK simply because we have and express our natural feelings; feelings as natural as breathing. But, you are OK. Remind yourself of this frequently. Some of the restraints that are placed on our bodies to be "good" are in direct conflict with a healthy body. Thus, the problem is not to reject the guides of religion, nor the guides of moralists, but to see if it's possible for each of you to work out for yourself a happy, comfortable and acceptable compromise. The purpose is to allow you to feel good about your feelings and about yourself, and to do this in line with your set of moral rules, whatever brand you happen to choose or were taught.

PEOPLE MAKE THE RULES

One of the things I think is important is to realize that your morals are given to you by people. Mothers, fathers, preachers, priests, rabbis, gurus, and people your age are all PEOPLE! Just as all the great books were written by PEOPLE! There are different sets of moralities — different sets of rules, held to fiercely by different people. The thing that most of us don't realize, especially when we are young, is that the set we happen to have may not be the *only set* nor the only "*right*" set. If you want to move towards being autonomous (self-naming), being self-determining or self-governed, becoming a person who is thinking for himself, then work now on developing your own set of ideals, values, and morals. These are very important for you. You must have them as automatic guides without having to think through each dilemma you encounter. So, if you feel that the values of your folks, your church, or your favorite guru are not for you, then start taking a look at what your own set of values are. Where did they come from? You weren't born with them. Who taught you? Did they do those people any good? If they did, then you can *begin* to look at how they will work for you.

MATURITY BEGINS HERE

This is where you begin to become a mature person. Blind acceptance of a set of rules keeps you in your Child. You are still saying, "Well, I'm just a little person and I have to take whatever grownups tell me and do it that way. I'm only OK if I do it their way." Well, that isn't quite true. You begin to become a responsible person when you begin to reason through what is good for you and the people you care about, what will keep you healthy, what will keep you mentally stable, emotionally OK, what will help you to feel OK, and be effective with the people you care about. This does not mean that we should throw away our religious teachings. I am saying that to become a responsible person, you must take a look at your religious learnings and see if they work for you, or if you can make them work and remain healthy. If they don't, and you can only give lip service to them (say you do but disobey the rules), they won't help you in times of stress. So, you must evolve a set of rules that will work for you. If they don't, maybe you don't fully understand them. Check this out with your religion teacher.

RELIGION MAY POINT THE WAY

There isn't *any* religion that can rightfully claim all wisdom, all truth, all the right answers. Right, good, and truth, like beauty, are in the eyes of the beholder. Some people claim divine inspiration and that is their privilege. Evidence to the contrary is found in the fact of the many contradictions between religions more than in their agreements. So, conflicts exist between what religions say. These often reflect the culture they serve. For example, one religion says the "savior" has been here and gone. Another says the "messiah" has not yet arrived. (We Jews open the door each year so he can come into our home during the Passover service.) One says pork is not good to eat and another says pork is OK, but fish is no good. Some religions idolize or worship nature; another has many deities (gods). Others believe there is only one God and He (chauvinism) is common to all. Maybe, when the truth is known, God will turn out to be a three-foot pygmy and she will be a woman. Who knows? Certainly not I. But I'm sure all the religions can't be completely right if there are so many differences. But religion helps as a guide in our behavior and there are many common rules which have survived for thousands of years. The Ten Commandments, for example, are usually found as basic to most religions and most laws. It's important for you to have some set of rules and follow them.

WHO IS RIGHT?

Who is to say, except for "*belief*" (subject to revision with the learning of new ideas), that one is more righteous, more moral, more free of sin? Who is healthier, the Eskimos, the primitive Indians, the old Hawaiians, the Trobriand Islanders, the South African Pygmies, the Europeans or Americans, or other so-called primitive cultures which seem to survive with a great deal more peace of mind and have healthier bodies than we do? For example, in the Trobriand Islands, the Igorot of Luzon, the Akamba of East Africa, and the Munski of northern Nigeria, there is a sex-positive attitude. Arrangements are made for adolescents to be together. There isn't any crime, insanity, neuroses, or any obesity among their tribes. This before-marriage liberty is a preparation for marriage. It allows a natural choice based on personality and compatibility rather than just sex appeal. Wilhelm Reich[20] states that following marriage, "both partners are remarkably faithful." Reich, in his *Discovery of the Orgone*, adds that a remarkable aspect of this premarital sexualtiy is its freedom from conception. Since the belief is held that there is no relationship between intercourse and pregnancy, girls do not get pregnant before marriage. Not so astounding when we think of the many childless couples in our own culture who adopt and then, with that permission and an increase in confidence in themselves to be parents, frequently conceive a natural child. The body knows.

97

RELIGION AND TA

Having said that, I'm sure I've aroused a lot of anger. I'm now going to say something else that I think may please a lot of people. TA places no guidance nor stress on you to reject *any* of your religious teachings. If your religious teachings work for you, and you are contented, healthy, and happy, for goodness sake, stay with them. Your Parent Tapes are protecting and helping you. That's what Parent Tapes are for — to protect and guide you. There is nothing that is more upsetting than to give up old ideals. However, one of the things I've found in transacting with group members is that some people get distorted ideas of what their religion teaches. They learn it only partially and then believe they've learned the total truth. They place unnecessary restrictions on themselves which can lead to both physical and mental breakdown. For these people, I can only recommend that in TA and in church you begin to explore with an open mind the things that are bothering you. You might talk with your minister or your counselor (or both) to see if you can work out a more relaxed attitude. You may have strong feelings of anger, fear, hurt, sex, or guilt. These are major feelings and are extremely powerful. To deny them, or to put them away so that you "don't have them" (which is what some people do in the name of "religion"), can indeed lead you to do some very peculiar things, outside of your awareness. You may try to shut off your Kid from your Adult because you're "not allowed to have such thoughts" according to your Parent. Your Parent may say, "Don't have them." So, your Child says, "All right. I give up. I won't feel them. I won't be aware of them." But they are there just the same. It's like putting a lid on a pot that's boiling and saying, "I'm going to act as if there's no pressure." This can only lead to one thing, and very frequently does.

*"You may try to put your unacceptable feelings away,
but they are there just the same."*

I   AM   NOT   AN-   GRY!

FEELINGS ARE NATURAL

Unfortunately, and unhappily, I've encountered in my life a number of wonderful young people who did exactly this. They took their supposedly unacceptable feelings of sex, anger, shame, guilt, or fear, put them away and said they weren't going to have them. They devoted all of their time to study and to "being good." Being good was being adaptive (AC) to what they thought their PICs were telling them. The reason they did this was because they didn't *think that there was any other way to make it.* There wasn't any other way to get life-giving strokes than to put away their own

98

feelings and let their important PIC's feelings count ("If I did that, my mother would be upset. If I did that, my father would kill me — or wouldn't like it. So I won't *feel* this way. I won't have these thoughts.") Some religion, and *your* morals. But let them be yours. I think that when we the moral rules of the church is immoral or sinful. I don't agree with that because *feelings are natural*. Repressing them is unnatural. The current wave of rebellion, failure, drop-out, crime, etc., maybe the direct result of discounting the feelings of people. So, I recommend that we don't repress and suppress feelings and thoughts, but that we learn to deal with them in a healthy, honest (authentic), and socially responsible way.

Then, what's a healthy way? Just do what you want, like an animal? No. One way is to talk about your feelings with a trusted and wise person. Not one with a bigger Parent than yours, but one who kind of "has it together," and can help you think and feel your way through your dilemmas. Each person has different feelings and concerns, different values and beliefs. That's why rules get broken.

WE NEED RULES

In any case, you need to have and be guided by your moral rules. Rules are guides for behavior. But, I think it is destructive and phony to act as if we didn't have feelings, to repress them out of our awareness until they build up to such an extent that we can't contain them. This can and does frighten us. Then, you see, we are into the conflict between *doing* what is "right," *feeling* good, and being healthy or ill. As a result of such conflicts, people get sick, think about or actually kill themselves or somebody else. Many are afraid of going crazy. Others run away. Don Juhl, who works with young folks on TA and Drugs says that "street people" call "runaways" "Fresh Meat" because they can use and abuse them. "Going crazy will resolve my problem," you may tell yourself, because then, "I won't have to feel guilty. I won't have to think about it anymore and I can let someone else take care of me." Not true. They don't "put you away" any more. And when you "go away" to an institution, you'll find you have to start figuring things out there.

KNOW YOURSELF

Being aware of your feelings now is important and makes much more sense. As a matter of fact, I've encountered a number of people in my practice who weren't able to resolve this. And in their late teens did one of the dire things I just described. *It isn't necessary to do that to yourself.* When all is said and done, we were never intended to go crazy, have a nervous breakdown, kill ourselves or someone else. There is no religion in the world that recommends that. No! We who feel OK enough to do work on our daily dilemmas would rather have you do anything else. As a matter of fact, one religion that I know says when you're sick, disregard your religions obligations and get well. Because your body is so very important, religion then takes second place to your health. So, nurturing yourself is very important. You can get back on the "right track," if you want to call it that, after you've calmed down some. *I think Parent Tapes, religious*

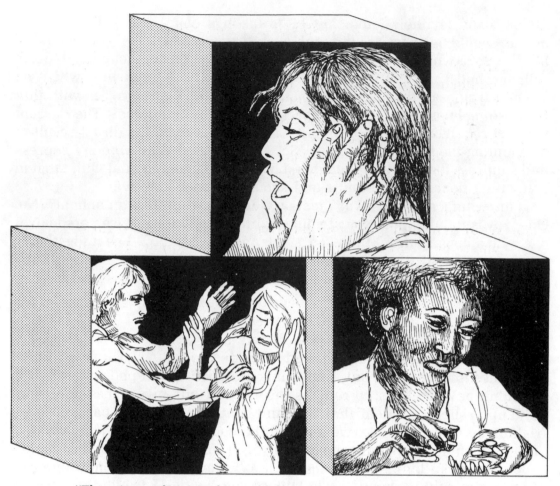

"There is no religion in the world that recommends that we go crazy, have a nervous breakdown, kill ourselves or someone else."

concepts of morality, values, and guides of behavior are extremely important for you. I think that you need to have a clear-cut understanding of them and that it is best to follow them most of the time. They give us feelings of safety in our life and they usually work pretty well. You don't get into so many hassles. You have less fun, perhaps, but also less trouble, and you come out with a more contented feeling about yourself and other people. Therefore, by and large, it's a good thing to have *your* values, *your* religion, and *your* morals. But let them be *yours*. I think that when we overstate them, when we deny our feelings, when we deny ourselves in the interest of God and say that God doesn't love us, or God is leaving us because we have natural feelings of love, of wanting to be touched, of wanting to have sex, then I think that we're being destructive and we need to take another look at our values.

QUESTIONS FOR YOUR ADULT

1. Are you puzzled about your values? Do you find yourself encountering people who don't believe in what you've been taught? Suppose what they say sounds OK; should you change? Listen? What? Talk about this in class.
2. Is talking to yourself crazy? Why? Why not? How can it help you?
3. Try writing down some of your confusions in your diary. Do you keep one? Lots of people find this very helpful for getting their thinking straight.
4. How can you be your own best friend?
5. What information do you get from your body? What do you feel when you are angry? What do you do? Swallow it? Express it verbally? Hit or break something? Run? Work? Wait till it goes away? Sulk? How do you handle your feelings?
6. What "old rules" do you believe in and follow? These are parent tapes. Are they like other people's?
7. How do social restraints affect your body? How will you handle this? What are your rules for behavior?
8. Discuss the idea that the "body knows."

EXERCISES (for your Kid)

1. Next time you're angry get a tennis racket or baseball bat and swat a mattress, or non-destructible pillow. When you do this say out loud, "I'm angry". Repeat this as many times as it takes to get the anger out.
2. To see if you are carrying "old brown stamps" (hidden anger) do Exercise 1 and keep it up till you feel the anger. Then keep on till you get it out. A good way to do this is to use an old rug on a clothes line. Remember to say "I'm angry". You may have to act your way into it at first. You'll know when it becomes real. Remember "you're OK to be angry."
   You're not OK to dump your anger on other people. That's hostility. Don't cry when you're angry. Yell.
3. Have you a place where you can scream? Find one and scream. You'll be surprised how good it feels. You're OK to scream.
4. Can you cry when you feel hurt? You're OK to cry, to feel sad. But watch your anger. Lots of people cover hurt with anger.
5. Tell someone you care about them, that you like them. Tell your folks about your feelings.
6. Have you a friend (someone who likes you), whom you trust? Share your feelings with your friend. Turnabout; be a good listener.

Chapter IX

THE HOOKERS AND YOU
(Parent Hookers, That Is)

"Conversation is a game of circles." Emerson

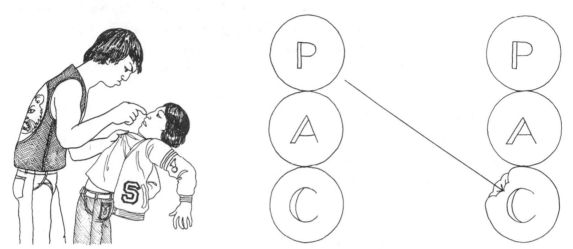

"PIC's often come on strong and act like "big men"."

One of the major complaints that boys and girls have about their mothers and fathers, teachers, the principal, policemen, and other such People In Charge (PIC) is that they "boss them around." PICs often come on strong and act like "big men," throw their weight around. As you know, in TA, we call that coming on Parent. In other words, they are letting their Critical Parent come on and tell you what's wrong with you. They tell you how and what to do and when to do it. This is very uncomfortable for you. You don't like being bossed, even "for your own good," and if some one person does this a lot, you begin to dislike that person very much.

PICs have been raised by other PICs. They have been trained to do just exactly what they're doing. It's like in the old days of hazing in college fraternities. Students who were hazed were newcomers, freshmen. They were called Rats, Plebes, or Frosh. They were often bullied, teased, and put down during their first year. Then, when they became sophomores, or second year men, they would take it on themselves to introduce the newcomers in the same way to the way of life in school.

THE GOOD OLD DAYS

The custom goes back even further, to English colleges, where they still have the "rat" system. There, a new student is taken on by an upperclassman as his servant and is treated almost as a slave. So, you see, there is a great deal of tradition attached to this. In a way, it gives sort of an authority or a license to PICs to make servants or chattels (a possession) of young people. Also, it places upon them the responsibility for your behavior and your training. So, they come on in a way that is intended, hopefully, to guide you into "correct" behavior. The purpose, supposedly, is to make it possible for you to live with them peacefully. But, that isn't what happens. Put-downs are rarely helpful. What you learn is how to put others down or to feel not OK about yourself. The bad part of this is, that since you're "one down," you're unable to do anything about your own life. A choice, other than complete rebellion, is to do what you're told without question by the PIC of your life.

All this gets mixed up with getting strokes. One of the things that we learn very early is, that if you want to get warm fuzzies or positive strokes, do what you're asked to do. If, then, you get the feeling that no matter what you do, you *can't* get strokes, you may do just the opposite to get bad strokes or cold pricklies. These are also life-supporting, but unpleasant. You get chewed out or hit, but you stay alive.

YOU MAY BE ASKING FOR IT

I have discovered that very frequently, without knowing it, some of us behave in such a way as to deliberately "bring on" the Parent in another person. Very frequently, the Person In Charge (PIC) would rather *not* come

"Some of us behave in such a way to deliberately "bring on" the parent of another person."

on in a strong, authoritarian way, but doesn't know how to avoid it. This is true whether it's at home or at work. There are things that employees, students, junior people, People Less In Charge (PLICs) will do which are guaranteed to "hook" the Parent of senior people (PIC). Now, this is OK if that is what you want (cold pricklies), but if you don't, knowing what some of these things are, especially with respect to the people whom you like, might get you out of that uncomfortable position of having a PIC coming down on you with their Parent. So, I've compiled a list of things that you may be doing to your Mother and Dad, teacher, boss, or other PIC which leads to their coming on Parent.

In a way, what I'm saying is that, while the responsibility for the way another person comes on is not yours (since you cannot respond for them), certainly the responsibility for your behavior, which results in their response, is *yours*, and you can do something about that. So, I've compiled this list. If you learn these so-called Parent Hookers, maybe you can avoid doing some of them. This could result in much more comfortable relationships between you and the PICs and OIPs* in your life.

There are a lot of things that I or others did as youngsters that really got our fathers or mothers mad. Wow! Did my mom come down on me when I told a lie or broke some furniture while "rough-housing" with my dog. Maybe you can think of some to add to the list. If you can, I'd sure like to have them because I'd like to share them with other people. Please send them to me. OK? Here's my list.

Complain

COMPLAIN

First of all, to get somebody to come on Parent, *complain.* If you complain, two things happen. The PIC will want to help you to change, or they'll tell you what to do to correct the thing that's bothering you. Now, you may not want to change at all. You may just want to complain. You may just want to let your feelings out and get a little sympathy. In that case, you get nurtured (rescued) by somebody's Parent. So, if you want to get somebody into their Parent, *complain* about anything. You're too warm; you're too cold; you're hungry; your foot hurts. Whatever. Just complain! You'll find that you'll have a lot of Parents around who are going to tell you how to fix it! what you should do, or shouldn't have done (I told you about running around in your bare feet).

*OIP (Other Important People)

105

Show Indecision

SHOW INDECISION

"I don't know what to do. I'm puzzled about this. I really can't make up my mind." When you do that, you're going to have other people "telling you what you should do." Now, if you don't want to be told what to do, then practice making decisions and staying with them. As we used to say in the Air Force, "Do something, even if it's wrong." Indecision creates a feeling of discomfort and insecurity in another person. So, when you're undecided, the other person's Kid gets upset. The PIC wants to feel safe, too, so he or she sets out to rescue you by telling you what to do. Thus, PIC's Parent tells *you* what to do so his or her Child can feel better. Therefore, if you want to hook another person's Parent, act in an indecisive way. You can't reach a decision. You're puzzled. You're confused. These kinds of things will undoubtedly result in somebody either rescuing you or putting you down. To avoid this, practice making decisions and standing by them. If you're wrong, you goofed. If you're right, you're a winner and not a little PLIC.

Ask For Criticism or Approval

ASK FOR CRITICISM OR APPROVAL

"Is this right? Am I doing it right? Is this good? Do you think this is okay?" In a childlike way, "Is this what you wanted me to do? Will this be all right?" In other words, a "How am I doing?" is bound to get a Parental response such as, "Oh! That's fine, son. You're doing a good job. However, (here it comes) I think you could do it better my way." Or, "everything's all right (gives strokes) except that part there which you always (ouch!) do incorrectly (takes them away), and you must remember, etc. . . . " (gives prickly). "How does this wall look (fresh paint)?" "It's beautiful (gives), but you missed three spots (takes away)." So, if you want to get that kind of stroke, fine with me. But remember, you asked for it! To avoid it, point out the defects and strengths and ask for what you want — like, "Tell me what you like about this."

107

Play Poor Me

PLAY POOR ME

"Things are awful. I feel terrible. Oh, my! This is wrong, that's wrong. Nobody likes me. They all pick on me." Playing "Poor Me" is saying, "Please feel sorry for me. Look at what a terrible life I lead." You're bound to get a lot of Parents rescuing you. Now, if your little Kid wants that kind of treatment, fine. You're enjoying life. You're getting goodies out of it. If you don't like it, however, remember you're setting yourself up to get Parented when you ask for pity. Sometimes you'll say, "Hey, Ma (to our own Parent), I'd rather do it myself. Get off my back." You don't have to say that to the other person. *Say it to yourself!* Of course, you may have played "Poor Me" *in order* to defeat your Rescuer. That's like the game, "What'll I do? Yes, but," that we mentioned earlier.

Ask For Advice

ASK FOR ADVICE

The most obvious one on the whole list is "Ask For Advice." If you ask for advice, you'll get it! Straight from the Parent. "What'll I do about my acne? My weight? My nails?" This is a set-up for a game of "What'll I Do? Why Don't You? Yes, But." The harder you play the WIDWDYYB game, the more angry or annoyed people get, and the more Parental advice you get. When you ask for advice, people think you really don't know the answer. Or, they think you do and must remind you, which in itself is a put-down. "I told you, etc. . . . " The other person may not know the answer either, but he has a lot of old-fashioned sayings to give you. For fat and overeating, *exercise your will power.* For nail biting, *paint bitter medicine on your nails.* For acne, *don't eat sweets or chocolate.* None of these will work, but you asked for it.

Platitudes (old wise sayings) are helpful at times. By the way, a platitude is something that Plato, the Greek Philosopher, is supposed to have said. The only trouble with Plato is that, if he said it several thousand years ago, it may or may not fit your dilemma right now. (He never heard of frozen nitrogen for skin treatment.) So, maybe a better way than using old platitudes is to begin to think, get accurate information, and figure things out for yourself. Now, that doesn't mean you always have to do it alone.* If you need more information, go to a reliable source: a teacher, counselor, books (more than one, please!). But, don't say, "I don't know." That's a cop-out. Most of the time, when you say, "I don't know," you're covering

109

over an "I don't want to say," or "I don't want to talk about it." That's straight. Check this out with yourself and see if, when you're saying, "I don't know," you don't mean, "I don't want to tell you." "I don't know" is a neat escape hatch. If you want to be truthful with yourself and other people, get out of the "I don't know" habit. Also, the "you know." Another way of copping out is the "You know" business. You know? You'll find you're coming on a lot straighter and avoid hooking the Parent of other people if you avoid "you know," "I don't care," or "I don't know."

Sigh "Oh Wow!"

SIGH! OH, WOW!

Okay. Here's some more. Did you ever come into the room, sigh, sit down, utter some statement like, "Oh, wow, (or she-it)" in a despairing voice? Then maybe you put your head in your hands, hold your head, or sit with your chin on your arms or stare straight ahead? This is a great performance; a great way to get Mom or Dad to say, "What's wrong, dear?" And, to get them hooked into their Parent. So, whatever goes down from then on is a result of that original bit of dramatic acting that you just put on.

Break Rules

BREAK RULES

Here's one that is a little more tricky. There are a set of rules and you know them, but you don't like them; like, don't smoke, or be in on time, or stop and turn in your work now. You know the rule. You just don't want to obey. You know how to wash the dishes. You know how to make the bed, or you know how to sweep the floor, be on time, get your work in when due. You've been taught this. It's just a drag to have to do what they say all the time! Maybe in school, it's the rule that you have to ask permission to visit the rest room. Maybe it's that you have to come in and take an assigned seat, but you want to sit next to an attractive friend. Whatever it is, you know the rule, but *you don't do it that way!* The greatest way I know to hook a Parent is not to do it the "right way." You wouldn't be too unhappy doing it according to the rule, but for one reason or another, you're doing it wrong. The real purpose may be to hook the Parent; to make the PIC angry. Check your Kid out, because if you're doing this, hooking Parents a lot, your Kid may be saying, "Hey! I need some strokes." There are better ways of getting strokes than that. What you're doing is setting it up so you'll get some uncomfortable kicks, put-downs, cold pricklies. Is it because you figure you can't get any other kind? Doing something against the rules may be because your Kid has a purpose that you don't know about: to get crooked strokes. To avoid this, turn on your Adult and figure out if that's what is going on. Another reason may be that you disagree

111

with the rule. To break it for that reason is dumb. Like not paying your taxes because you disagree with the mayor of your town and wind up in jail. Well, if you like being a martyr, OK.

Be Cruel

BE CRUEL!

Another hooker is to be cruel to people, especially to younger or weaker people. You know, there's an old Parent Tape that says, "Boys mustn't hit girls." "Big mustn't hit little." "You shouldn't hit little or weaker people." "Girls shouldn't hit people who are weaker or smaller." I mean, everyone knows that. It's a given. No matter what your culture or your generation, you're taught to protect younger, smaller, or weaker people. So, when you pick on a younger or weaker person, you're bound to hook everyone else who goes by that rule, and most people do. If you want to hook somebody, do something cruel or rough that's going to endanger a younger or weaker person, and you'll bring out the Parent. I'm not telling you not to do it. I'm just saying that if you want to hook a Parent, that's what to do.

112

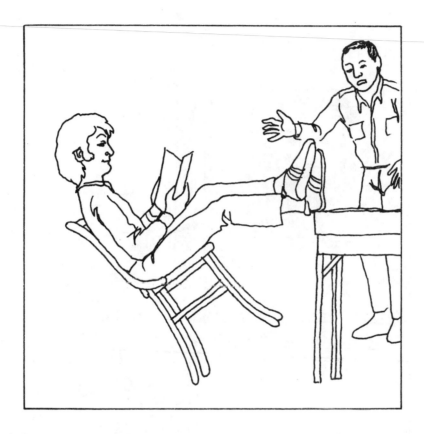

Endanger Yourself

ENDANGER YOURSELF

Another way to get Parents to tell you what to do or not to do is to do something to endanger yourself. That usually brings on the Rescuer Parent in most people, especially those who care about you. For one thing, they hate to see you hurt. They don't like you to be hurt because your parents love you and what hurts you upsets them. What's even worse, if you get hurt, it's usually Mother or Dad that will have to take care of you while you heal. So, the way to bring out a rescuer, or even a Critical Parent, is to do something that endangers you, something which will necessitate their taking steps to prevent you from doing this dangerous, hazardous thing, or in their having to rescue (hospital, juvie, etc.) you.

113

Destroy Things of Value

DESTROY THINGS OF VALUE

Another way is to destroy something that the owner wants or likes, or something that they've given you. That's a way to hurt someone, and also to bring out their Parent. Parents may say, "Waste not, want not." That's an old Parent Tape. You may not have heard it, but it means if you don't waste it, you won't have to want for things later.

Okay? There are a lot more of these. I'm sure you've thought of a dozen of them while I've been going on here. I'll just name some others and you'll probably understand them without my spelling them out.

114

Wrinkle Up Your Nose

WRINKLE UP YOUR NOSE

That's a good one for getting people mad and hooking them.

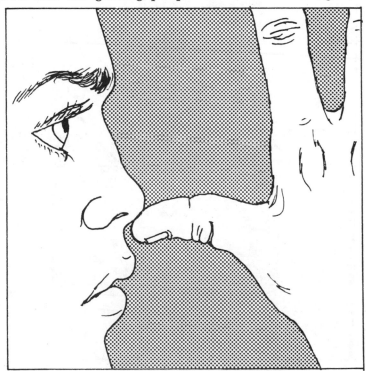

Put Your Thumb to Your Nose

PUT YOUR THUMB TO YOUR NOSE

This is a derisive gesture. Know what it means?

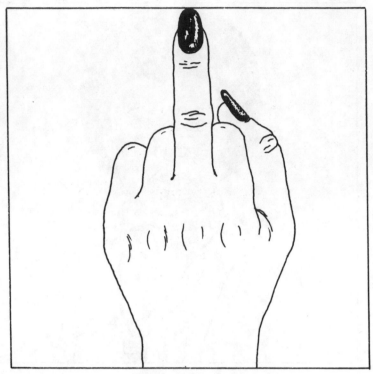

Middle Finger in the Air

MIDDLE FINGER UP IN THE AIR

Flick-off is a good one for bringing down Parents on you.

Spilling Things

SPILLING THINGS

Doing this over and over indicating carelessness. Could be a game called "Schlemiel" (Stupid or Clumsy).

Laughing too Loudly

LAUGHING TOO LOUDLY

Especially in a library, or school room, so it's jarring to people.

Don't Answer

DON'T ANSWER

One of the best ones I know for hooking a Parent is *when a PIC speaks to you and you don't answer.* You act as if they weren't there and look away.

117

If they persist, you can also come up with "Oh! were you talking to me?" That usually gets an added bonus of more exasperation from them.

Playing Stupid

PLAYING STUPID

"Stupid" is like when somebody says, "Would you please sweep the floor?" You answer, "Floor? How do I sweep the floor?" "With the broom, stupid." "Broom? Where? I don't see any broom?" Okay. Then you get the broom and you say, "Okay, what am I supposed to do with this?" The longer you keep playing this, the more angry they get until they come down with their big Parent (or do it themselves, which is the purpose of your game). The broom-floor bit was an example of how the game of "Stupid" is played. Play it enough and you can "get out" of anything - school, your home, the service, your job, and so on. You probably know that you're doing this. You might be doing it to get their goat, but you're also hooking their Parent, and punishment is uncomfortable.

Don't Finish Your Job

DON'T FINISH YOUR JOB

Another way is to *not finish a job that you've taken on*. People who are older usually believe in finishing a task they start. It's an old Chinese Proverb! (Parent Tape?) Hopefully, they have taught you this. They know that you know it. They hope that you're as much concerned about the task as they are. So, one way to indicate that you don't give a darn about them (which is also designed to hook them) is not to finish it; leave it half done. A popular game, built on this, is called IDIWIGDGAR. ("I'll Do It When I'm Darned Good And Ready.")

119

Hair

HAIR

In recent years, we've engaged in a battle of the hair. Now, most people grow hair any way they want. If they choose, they can let it grow long, whether they be male or female, and no one is very concerned. Long hair can be beautiful, or it can be a mess. Most PICs now admire, or at least don't mind, long hair. It has taken a long time to win this battle. Do you remember when the Beatles first came over here? They were considered *ridiculous* (Parent word) to the older generation when all good Americans were wearing a crewcut. Now, here *they* come with hair down to their shoulders, over their eyes. Well, from that day to this there's been a long *growing* (that's a pun) period. People have come a long way in their thinking, so that most people now can see that long hair is not that destructive. In fact, it's kind of attractive. With hair styling and so on, it's kind of neat. But, what no one will accept (you can hear my Parent talking) is somebody that just lets it grow and be dirty and disheveled. Being dirty may be OK with you, not bathing may be OK with you, being smelly may be OK with you, but it isn't OK with lots of other people. Because it's offensive. So, being dirty and sloppy is something that is going to hook many PICs. Yes, you'll still hook an old-fashioned PIC just with long hair, too. If you want to hook Parents, just go around without bathing, looking sloppy, doing disgusting things with your nose, and so on.

Other Parent hookers include the games of "Where's My," "Mom, she or he took my favorite . . . " "Keysar!" (D'yaknowheremykeysar?).

120

Now, here are a whole bunch of things that I've mentioned. I'm sure that you can think of dozens more, of how to get your Mother, Father, or teacher mad. You can probably dream up a bunch of your own. It isn't so good for them, and it won't be so good for you. but, if you insist on doing it, at least be aware of what you're doing. The thing that's pathetic to me is when you do these things, the wrath descends on you and you innocently wonder, "What'd I do? How come everyone got mad at me? I didn't do anything. I was just sitting here, minding my own business (and humming)." OK?

So, if you're going to do things that you know Mothers, Dads, teachers, and bosses (and wives) disapprove of, *expect* their Parent to come on. If, on the other hand, you don't like their Parent, you'll know how not to hook them.

The best way to keep people out of their Parent is to stroke their Kid. The next best way I can recommend for keeping other people out of their Parent is to avoid doing things that are going to put them into their Parent. I think that each of us has some responsibility for that because with TA, we're much more knowing about how other people are; if we think about it, if we care about them and about ourselves.

QUESTIONS FOR YOUR ADULT

1. Do you feel bossed around? By whom? Tell an incident where this happened. Do you do any Parent Hooking?
2. What are you Parent Hookers?
3. What can you do to get out of the Parent Hooking business?
4. Is Parent Hooking limited only to your folks? Who else?
5. Can you tell the difference between a Critical Parent and a straight Adult statement? Give an example.
6. Is doing what you're asked to do a put-down for you? Why? Check this out to see if you are coming on rebellious Child.
7. When you were left in charge of someone, did they ever force you to come on Critical Parent?
8. What's your Nurturing Parent like? Are you a rescuer? Kind and loving? Do you compliment people? Tell them how well they're doing?
9. Did any of the Parent Hookers in the chapter remind you of yourself or someone else? Talk about this.

EXERCISES

1. Have a role playing session in class or group where you act out one or more Parent Hooking situations. Then discuss how this could be handled productively.
2. Make a list of Parent Hookers not in the chapter.
3. Think of ways to stroke the Kid of a PIC. Do it. Then check how it feels. Compare that with the strokes you get through Parent Hooks.

IDEAS AND WORDS TO FIND OUT ABOUT

1. PIC's. People or persons in charge.
2. Rats, plebe, and frosh. First year people in high school or college. These are terms intended to make fun of or to discount the new student.
3. PLIC's. People less in charge who have some authority over you and use it to please themselves.
4. OIP. Other important people in your life.
5. Platitudes.
6. Philosopher.
7. Derisive gestures. One such gesture is the well know flick-off (middle finger pointing towards sky.) Showing great lack of respect for the other person towards whom it is directed.
8. Schlemeil: A German word meaning stupid or clumsy fellow. TA people use it to describe a Game. Do you every play this?

Chapter X

ASIA: THE GOALS OF TA

Out of the stuff of dreams
come the facts of science . . . AMF

AUTONOMY (A) - SELF-DETERMINATION

The young people and elders whom I've known like to feel that they have something to say about what happens to them. That they are not just being told what to do. The idea that our lives are planned out and that, therefore, we are fated to become whatever someone has told us we are is unpleasant. I was once told, "You're going to grow up to be President of the United States." For a long time, I believed that until I found out how impractical that idea was. But, I still had some big-shot ideas about myself until I began to get things more in line with my abilities and interests. Many of us are programmed (scripted) with a self-fulfilling prophecy. We are

"Many of us are programmed with self fulfilling prophecy."

125

told, "You are never going to be worth a darn," or "You'll be a failure," or "You're stupid." So we give up working on goals. Or, "You are probably going to be an athlete when you grow up. You may not be much in arithmetic, but you sure can hit a baseball." Thus, we get programmed into being athletes and not scholars. Or the other way around. We're told, "You're not much in athletics; you're a physical moron, but you are a great scholar. Your thing is thinking. Don't worry about the jock kind of thing because it's not for you." Girls are frequently told that they'll grow up to be great mothers and housewives. Maybe this isn't what they really want. But *they* decide to accept the prophecy. What you can do with TA is free yourself from self-imposed failure scripts (life plan prophecies) and decide for yourself what you want to do, be, and have. Through TA, we're attempting to help you develop skills in being "self-governing" or autonomous (pronounced: AW-TAHN-eh-MUSS). And that's really what you want, isn't it? To be independent, able to think and decide your life for yourself. OK? But think (A), not feel (C).

LETTING YOUR KID OUT - SPONTANEITY (S)

Another goal in TA is *spontaneity* (pronounced: SPON-(sounds like Ron)-TAN-AY-ITY). You are spontaneous when you let your free Kid out. Spontaneity is impulsive, spur-of-the-moment behavior — being free to let go and feel. Free to have and to express your own feelings; not to be ashamed or embarrassed or shy. Spontaneity is having and expressing your body feelings, feelings of love and affection for other people, anger, fear, or hurt. In spite of your early teachings, you need not be ashamed of, nor embarrassed by, these feelings. Many of us go through life keeping our feelings deep inside of us and denying to ourselves and others that we have them. This makes it difficult or impossible to love and be loved, to have fun, to laugh or experience joy in life. In America, we wrongfully place a great deal of value on keeping a calm exterior*. We probably have the greatest

"In America we wrongfully place a great deal of value on keeping a calm exterior."

*Look how we reward Henry "Fonzi" Winkler, John Wayne, Humphrey Bogart and David Janssen for their great stone-faced acting ability.

number of ulcers and the greatest amount of high blood pressure of any nation on earth because we keep our feelings hidden. We are taught, "Keep your feelings to yourself. Don't talk back!" We sulk and pout so as not to express our anger. We don't know how to relieve ourselves of the tensions that develop, so we remain "nervous." When we do this, we say we are tense, nervous, up-tight. Being "nervous" is keeping your feelings in by tensing your muscles. This keeps you "uptight." So, if you want to avoid being nervous, do something physically active (not violent). Also, say what you are feeling - talk about your feelings and you'll find that you feel a lot better.

The second goal of TA, then, is to be *spontaneous*; to be able to act on impulse (act on a feeling); to let feelings out; to do the things that feel good at the time. Of course, from a practical and moral point of view, we must keep in mind the possible results and be willing to accept responsibility for our behavior. In other words, "make sense, man." But always following rules and always playing it safe keeps your Kid dull and depressed. Those who lack spontaneity are usually dull and boring to others. Spontaneity is a delightful quality of fun, of honest laughter, of joy. Being able to feel, to express anger or hurt, or to be excited and to be a person endears us to others.

Out of the stuff of dreams come the facts of science and invention. Spontaneity is permission and ability to daydream. Give yourself permission to dream, imagine, fantasy, make-believe. And then get to work. Inventions are one percent inspiration (dream) and 99 percent (work). (And that's not imagination, people.)

CONTRACTS AND INTEGRITY (I)

Integrity is a quality of moral honesty, strictness in fulfillment of contracts, of trustworthiness, of truthful behavior. It is the essence of contracts between people and nations. It is a basic goal of TA. Contracts are essential in any kind of relationship between you and another person. A contract in which each has had an equal opportunity to work it out is more likely to succeed. It is a statement that you will do something and the other person agrees that this is okay with them and that they will, in turn, do something that is also acceptable to you. A good contract provides a basis for understanding each other. It sets the rules. If you have agreed to a set of rules and each of you always follows your rules, you know you can depend on the other person to do what you think he is going to do. If you don't have a contract, there is no agreement and no basis for getting along. If you frequently find yourself in conflict, fighting or arguing, you may not have a clear contract. When people say, "You said," or You promised," or "You're not fair!" or "You are cheating," and so on, the trouble may be because of a lack of a contract or because you assumed there was a contract. Without a contract, friends and family members often wind up with lots of bad feelings, lots of brown stamps, frozzies - unpleasant or unhappy feelings. But contracts are not orders. They are agreements drawn up by and between *consenting* people. If it's one-sided, it's a dictated rule and may not work.

John F. Whittaker, in a paper called *OK Street Work Fun Book* states a number of good ideas related to contracts. He says that first of all, *a contract is based on wanting to belong with another person, not having to belong to them.* This also means that you want to be together, but not necessarily to be united as one person. You can stay separate and maintain your own individual personality. It means that when you have a contract, it is *clearly* stated, and is based on the *understanding* that *you will* (and you agree to this) *keep the contract.* You will always have the opportunity then, if you find that the contract isn't working, or it's too restrictive for you, to change it at some other time by mutual agreement.

LOOK, SINCE WE HAVE A CONFLICT, LET'S MAKE A CONTRACT ABOUT USING THE PHONE.

O.K. YOU LEAVE THE PHONE IN OUR ROOM THE HELL ALONE AND USE THE ONE IN THE DEN FROM NOW ON!!

"Never make a contract when you are angry."

Never make a contract when you are angry. You, or the other person, will be using power in an oppressive way. You will make the contract too strict for the other person, or too one-sided, and they may agree to it out of fear. So, don't make contracts when you are angry.

SOMETHING FOR EACH

Make sure that both people get something out of it. Then it isn't a one-sided contract. If each person gives something because he cares about the other person, the contract will work out well.

Remember that (1) contracts are not made just one way. That
(2) each gets something out of it and also gives up something;
(3) that you can rework the contract if it doesn't work out, and
(4) not to make it when you are angry.

Another important thing to remember about contracts is that
(5) *they should deal with a simple thing,* like taking turns doing chores. But not too simple. In that way, you can work on something important to you both.

(6) The contract should be limited to one thing; not a whole lot of things. If you make one contract work, then you can make more contracts because you'll have confidence and trust in yourself and the other person. The Nazi government in Germany was notorious for making and breaking treaties and contracts. This resulted in World War II when it was apparent that we couldn't deal with them. Keeping contracts, for this reason alone, is essential. Think how it would have affected our relationship with Germany if there had been a long history of integrity, of dependable behavior under

law. Integrity is the basis for all trust between people and is built on conformity to mutually-agreed-upon rules of behavior. Thus, TA suggests you build integrity by following the rules to which you've agreed. If you don't like the rule, work on rewriting it and getting agreement. But obey it until it's changed. That's integrity.

AUTHENTICITY (A)

Authenticity (Aw-then-tiss-it-ee) means being genuine or real. When you are coming on straight, being truthful, people learn to rely on what you say, to depend on your doing what you say you will do . . .

When you are being honest, you are game free. People learn they can depend on what you promise. "His word is as good as his bond," is an old saying meaning he has integrity and is authentic.

To be authentic takes lots of Adult strength. To become authentic you must practice sticking to your promises, your agreements, your rules, and your moral code. Even when it hurts you to do so. Our Kid often wants to do what it feels like doing even though we may have agreed to something else. When you keep the contract you strengthen your Adult and become more authentic. In other words you're "for real." Two authentic people are more likely to make it in a relationship than are those who play games.

Thus TA has four goals; authenticity, spontaneity, integrity, and autonomy. (ASIA). Perhaps with these you can begin to form a set of rules for living in a society where the old rules don't fit and new ones are, to say the least, not yet wholly endorsed by a majority of the population.

QUESTIONS FOR YOUR ADULT

1. What are the four goals of TA? Explain them.
2. How have you used them this week?
3. Discuss them. Do they fit for you? Do you feel ripped off when you follow them and others do not? What do you think you should do about that?
4. What is a self-fulfilling prophecy? Have you had any laid on you? What can you do about it? How can you change your life script? Can you use any of the "goals" to help you?
5. Are you spontaneous? Do you have fun? How can you plan for fun? Do you ever do anything on impulse? Why not? Do you wish you could? What's preventing it?
6. Can you tell somebody to "be spontaneous"? Can they do it? Why not?
7. What are some important things about contracts?
8. In any relationship there is a contract, even though it is not stated. How come? Do you have any inferred contracts? Do they work? Any disappointments? How can you change this?
9. Are ASIAN characteristics born in you? Can you develop them? How?

EXERCISES

1. Practice making decisions and sticking to them. Then review the decision and decide if it was right. If not, form a new rule.
2. Practice making contracts at home with your OIP's. Then review the contract one week later to see how it worked. Stay with the agreement until review time, then change it if necessary.
3. Look for areas of disagreement at home. Try to get people to make contracts which will smooth things out. Don't give up too easily. Remember "Losers try. Winners do."
4. Make some contracts in school, with teacher, counselor, or friends. Check in one week and one month to see how they worked out.

IDEAS AND WORDS TO LEARN MORE ABOUT

1. Autonomy
2. Spontaneity
3. Integrity
4. Authenticity
5. Contracts
6. Being "nervous"

Chapter XI

LEADERSHIP AND TA GOALS

"You must look into people as well as at them." Chesterfield

"Maybe you did nice things, then felt like you had been ripped off."

RESCUER OR VICTIM

Many times in the past you have heard ministers, teachers, parents, and other PICs not only expressing their own ideas, but quoting from the Bible or other religious documents about doing good things for people: "cast your bread on the waters," "be kind to other people," "be a good Samaritan," and the like. Then, maybe you tried it and things didn't work out just exactly as they had promised. You did the nice things, and then you felt like you had been ripped off because they took advantage of your so-called good nature. In the meantime, you've watched others whom you didn't admire, whom you thought were pretty poor specimens, get elected to jobs in school leadership or be appointed to positions that you felt you could do better, such as president of the class, or captain of the team, or whatever. Each time, perhaps, that you've gone into a new group, you've wondered, "Now, how do I go about getting the group to like me? How do I get them to elect *me* to a position of leadership? How can I be recognized as the kind of person that's outstanding?"

There have been many books written on leadership, and while lots of people have read them, there continues to be only a small number of people who are in positions of leadership. Did you know that in our U.S. Senate

133

there are only 100 Senators and, of course, there is only one President of the United States? There are only 50 Governors, and so on. Now, how does the world select these people to be heads of government? How did little Napoleon get so big? How did Winston Churchill make it?

THREE QUALITIES TO WIN BY

Many years ago, a study was made to find out what makes people leaders. What are the qualities of leadership? The researcher listed many personality traits. They included being pleasant, showing initiative and originality, push, hard work, intelligence, talent, good scholarship, tallness, physical attractiveness, and so on. Some of you cynics might say bribery or brown-nosing. This list included two or three hundred of these so-called traits that people who are leaders sometimes exhibit. They included all of the character goals of the Boy Scouts, like trustworthy, loyal, helpful, friendly, courteous, and so on. The research team tested these traits, one against the other, and one against all. They did what is called in statistics, a factor analysis.

When they were all finished with these tests, there were only three factors which were typical of most of the leaders selected for study. The three qualities were *competence* (able to do the job), an *ability to help the group achieve its goals*, and *personal pleasantness*. These don't seem so startling. Yet, if you will evaluate the people who are presidents of your class, or the leaders of your groups, you may find that they possess these qualities and characteristics. And they are qualities you can acquire. No one is a born leader.

COMPETENCE

First of all, whatever it is they are doing, leaders have to know how to do it well, or have to learn how very rapidly. It's true that sometimes we elect people to positions of leadership because they personally are fun to be around, but then they are not able to do the job. Sometimes we elect people who are bright, but they aren't much fun and we don't want to follow what they tell us, even though they are right. If you'll take a look at some of the people around school who are in student body government (the wheels), you'll find that they probably have some of these characteristics.

These characteristics — competence (ability to perform the task well), pleasantness, and understanding what the group wants - aren't inherited. You can develop them. The idea of being competent means that you have to know how to do whatever it is that you must do. If you want to conduct a meeting, it's important that you know Robert's Rules of Order and that you are able to stand up in front of a group and make sense. You don't necessarily have to have "good English," but if you wish to make yourself understood, you must be able to speak effectively.

GROUP GOALS

Of more importance is understanding what the group wants, where the group wants to go, and then helping them to get there. Years ago, President

*"If you look at the people who are in student government,
they probably have common characteristics."*

Franklin D. Roosevelt told the country, "If you want to recover from this depression, follow me. I'll help you. I know how." So, the country elected him (four times). Whether his solutions then were good for the country only history can tell us. But, he did provide us leadership at a time when leadership was crucial to us.

CHARISMA

One of the additional things about Franklin Roosevelt which seemed to appeal to most people then was a quality also present in John Kennedy. That was the feeling of warmth and pleasantness he exuded. Both of them gave us the feeling that they were self-confident, felt good about themselves, and felt good about us, the people, and knew what we wanted. It was that joviality, that fun feeling that so endeared both of them to us. Regardless of their competence, regardless of whether they were right or wrong, people loved them as perhaps few people have been loved throughout history. Of course, there were some people who hated President Roosevelt for some of his policies, but there were very few people who disliked him as a person. (He *was* elected four times.) Of course, whether he was so loved individually, in private life, is hard to know. But, as leaders, Roosevelt and Kennedy are outstanding examples of being pleasant, competent, and able to unite us in a cause. They had "charisma." From these come a generalized feeling of dedication to our country and unity to ourselves and with the leader.

Those are three qualities of leadership. How does one go about learning them? Well, some of the things we talk about in TA will help. Turn on your Adult, learn the things you need to know to help the group do what it wants to do! For example, if your class wants to win an election, find out what they will need in order to do it and provide some of the information. Finding out where the group wants to go in terms of accomplishing whatever it is they need is very important. Most important of all is letting people know you think they are worthwhile, important, and adequate (OK), and that you care about them. A feeling of OKness results when people feel understood and accepted.

SOME GOALS

Probably one other quality is very important. Reassure the group that you and they have the same beliefs and wants, and that you can help them achieve their goals. Reassure the People In Charge that you will obey the rules (in school or in the community), while you are functioning as a leader, because it's difficult for official PICs to approve of so-called new ideas if the new ideas threaten rules which protect people and make them feel safe. They need new thinking and innovations, and they applaud initiative and inventiveness to solve problems. These are your contributions as a leader. Through new and exciting approaches to old problems, a leader can generate movement where others failed. But, there is a current need for stability in our organizations, at home, school, or state, the lack of which frightens us and leads to resistance to change. This is called conservatism. People In Charge (PIC) need to know that old values and old morals are not going to be ignored while we are making changes in ways of doing things. This, more than anything else, is the so-called generation gap. The generation gap is the failure on the part of both groups, new and old, to accept the fact that each will be treated fairly and will be protected through any change. When PICs see people in high school or college flaunting rules of administrative morality, integrity and law, they become frightened. When young people see no movement to change, no acceptance of their feelings, they become angry.

AUTHENTICITY — FOR REAL

One of the basic goals of TA is to help you become authentic; straight with yourself and others. Strive to make sense to yourself and other people. Thus, we believe it isn't necessary to flaunt the old rules in the interest of finding a new way of solving problems. This, by no means, indicates that you have to do it the way it's always been done. What we're all looking for are new and better ways of solving old problems. We PICs recognize and admit readily that we haven't solved all the dilemmas, all the difficulties of the world. We have solved some of them, and we don't want to lose what

"PIC's are afraid to let go of some of the things they've learned because they work well for them."

we've paid such a high price to learn. We are afraid to let go of some of the things that we've learned because we know that they have worked pretty well for us, and have kept some of us from going back to the jungle.

For instance, civilization has gone through centuries of turmoil under tyranny and dictatorship - dating back to medieval times. We do not wish to have to reexperience this because our democracy is not all we would wish it to be. So, when your PICs don't jump as rapidly as you would like into a "radically new way," drop out of your idealistic Kid long enough to listen to the other side, i.e., traditional values, beliefs, ideals, and the like.

137

AMERICA'S VALUES ARE OK

There's little wrong with the American value system. But, making it work takes being *authentic* (honest), being *autonomous* (standing up on your own two feet and expressing what you believe), having *integrity* (truth, honesty, straight), and being *spontaneous* (able to be enthusiastic, get excited, love yourself and others), and being able to see the humor in the whole thing.

These are the qualities that TA develops. Thus, TA can be the way to strengthen our "way of life," and to assist others to achieve similar goals. Maybe, I'm OK — You're OK means everybody in the world. What do you think?

QUESTIONS FOR YOUR ADULT

1. What are the three main qualities that the chapter states are necessary to be a leader? Who do you know that has these qualities? Are they leaders?
2. What are PIC's afraid of when "radical leaders" take over? How can a new leader get their support and cooperation?
3. Discuss the idea, "There's little wrong with the American value system. But, making it work takes being authentic, autonomous, and spontaneous and having integrity."
4. Do you agree that "Everybody is OK"? Why or why not?

EXERCISES

1. Select a school problem and "brainstorm" for solutions in class. Brainstorming means open discussion. Everyone tries to suggest all the possible solutions they can think of. Everything that is said is recorded (on the chalkboard or on paper). No one corrects or criticizes what is said.
2. After the brainstorming session, put your Adults to work to select a few workable ideas.
3. Divide the class into groups to implement the solutions chosen.
4. Try this same process at home — or in a club group.
5. List the leaders in your school and list the characteristics that made them leaders.

IDEAS AND WORDS TO LEARN MORE ABOUT

1. Competence
2. Charisma

Chapter XII

HASSELTIMES AT HOME
Or, Taking Out the Garbage and Other Dilemmas of Living With People

"Keep cool, anger is not argument."   *Daniel Webster*

"Fights at home with people you love often occur at the same time every day."

TELEPHONE AND TA

There are times, at home, when you get into fights with the people you love. Then you wind up feeling angry or frozzy, and so do they. If you think of TA at the time, you'll have a better chance to stay out of the fights and feel better. These hassles often occur at the same time evey day - like in the morning, before dinner or at dinner or before bedtime. If you can determine when they occur, that's a first step in avoiding them. So look for Hassletimes*.[22] You'll find it will help to know a little about TA games, because many of the things we'll talk about here are based on "games." TA games are a series of transactions which we do over and over again, in the same way; things we say to the same people, that usually result in our being upset with each other. Then we always wind up being either mad or sad, hurt or silent, sick and feeling gypped.

THE GARBAGE GAME

Fights at home usually start over the same thing. For example, mothers and dads frequently come to consult with me about their son who "won't take out the garbage." I've told such mothers and fathers that I make more

141

money as a psychologist out of *garbage* than I do from almost any other problem. So, "taking out the garbage" is one of the things I would like to talk about. Another is use of the *telephone.* Who gets to use it, how long, rights of all, etc. Then rules for dating, *staying out late,* and other hassle-homers. How can you handle yourself when you have to bring a *bad grade* home? And also, how can you get along better on a *job?* What about *drugs?* What can you do when other people are using them and you're there? What about this thing of falling in *love?* I can hear you giggle about that, because every time I mention love in group, somebody starts to laugh, feel silly and embarrassed, etc. But you do fall in love and are embarrassed about it. If you talk about it you'll find others feel the same way.

What about *friends?* Do you get along with friends, and how do you get to be friends, and how do you *"keep friends?"* What is a friend?

How do you get Mom to *stop bugging you?* How do you stop her from telling you not to do something which you have no intention of doing, but which she is afraid you will do, and which, if you did, could get you into trouble? These are fairly common questions which, when handled in traditional ways, wind up in some very unhappy situations. I'm sure some of you encounter the problem of getting into a *fight* with *Dad,* or *Mom,* over and over, and never knowing how it started, why it started, or who started it. Really, the only thing you know is that it wound up very unpleasantly. These are some of the things we are going to talk about in this chapter.

USING THE DON AMECHE* (Short for Telephone)

Let's start with the Telephone — TA and the Telephone. There is probably nothing that is more fun, in everyday life, than being able to get on the phone and talk to a friend of yours across the city or across the country. Everybody enjoys it. The telephone is a useful gadget for calling for help, to find out what chapter to study, how to do algebra problem #6, or what happened when. It is also used in business to communicate quickly and easily. Men and women can make agreements on the telephone which have far-reaching effects. The telephone use in the home has changed in my lifetime from being a novelty and luxury, to being an essential part of living in a social world where friends live so far apart. Part of this is due to our very different transportation (cars, and so forth).

When I was young, not everybody had a telephone, and if you wanted to use one, you either went next door or across the street to the neighbors, or you went down to the corner drugstore where there was a pay telephone. You put a nickel in, and you could make a telephone call. For a long, long time, telephone calls at home were limited in number and length of call. You weren't allowed to make more than two or three calls a day without having to pay extra money for them. One of the nice things about telephones now is, that we can usually make as many calls as we want, for as long as we want and for free. Now that you are older, a teenager, you

*The Don Ameche is old slang for Telephone. Don Ameche was a Hollywood star who took the role of Alexander Graham Bell in a hit movie some years before you were born.

have friends, acquaintances, and business (school activities, part-time jobs and the like). You have lots of things you need to talk to people about.

At home, when I wanted some information about my homework, I would get on the phone and talk for a long time. My folks were very patient. They would allow me to go on sometimes for an hour or two doing algebra or chemistry with a friend. Neither one of us knew how to do it, and with our pooled ignorance, we really didn't find out either, but we enjoyed being stumped together and reassuring each other "this is crazy." It seemed like the reasonable thing to do at the time. My folks weren't too concerned about this, because it didn't happen all the time, and my regular use of the telephone was perhaps limited to a shorter period in the evening. I was an only child and, therefore, if Mother or Dad had wanted the telephone, they would have said, "Alvyn, finish that up. I need to make a telephone call." It wasn't terribly important if people didn't call us, because our business didn't depend on a call. Of course, we never did know what calls we didn't get — we might have been getting a call from the local radio station (no TV in those days. Sounds like the dark ages, doesn't it?) telling us that we had won $64.00, (not $64,000, like now.) and we'd have never known it.

TIME SHARING

In those days, it was a little bit different. One of the pains you feel at home is when you want to use the telephone, and somebody is on it. Or, you're on it, and you have to get off because Dad wants it. Now, the telephone is a very important thing to everyone in the family. Dads, mothers, brother and sisters (if you have them), grandmother, whoever lives at your house, have business acquaintances or friends who need to call them. Since the telephone is important to everyone, and everyone enjoys it, it becomes a matter of how much time each person can have on the telephone. To refer back to an earlier chapter we talked about contracts. Making a contract to use the telephone is a fairly simple matter.

"Making a contract is a fairly simple matter."

143

Without one, the telephone can be the source of lots of anger and frustration at your house. Making a contract requires a set of rules, understandings and trust. The *trust* is that people will honestly try to live up to it. The *understanding* is that when it doesn't work, it's not because of a "cheater," but because maybe the contract had some weakness, is unfair, impractible (no good), and needs to be changed.

The rules for making a contract are:

1. Never make a contract when you or your folks are angry. (It won't be fair).

2. When making a contract, limit your talk about it to 15 minutes.

3. *Limit the talk to one simple topic*, i.e., telephone, garbage, the car, allowance, etc. Avoid many topics. Make one contract work first, then do another. Success builds trust and confidence. If Dad says he'll do something and does it, you'll trust him on the next thing. If you live up to your agreement, the next contract will be easier to make.

4. Be open. There's more than *one way* to meet your needs. Keep in mind your people love you, and are trying to live more happily with you. They care about you and aren't trying to gyp or fool you. Keep in mind where they are too. (4, 5, 6, remember)? Remember, they are trying to get used to your new need for freedom. It scares them. So take it easy in your early demands. You'll get more, later, easier, if you're reasonable now.

5. Consequences Clause. What happens if someone doesn't do what you agree on? Don't go for punishment here, but describe unpleasant consequences, i.e., too long on the telephone, you lose your next turn.

6. Give because you love, not to get. In business contracts, you "give to get." In a family contract, you give because you care about others and they you. Yield a little to others' wants.

7. Make sure each person comes away with a good feeling. Each should get something he wants and give up something.

8. Stay in your Adult when figuring things out. Parents are too bossy or generous and Kids too demanding or agreeable.

9. Write down your agreement and read it out loud.

10. Plan to review how it's working in one week.

OK. Now we know how to make a contract. Try it out. How much time do you need to talk with your friends? Should telephone conversations be limited to three minutes, five minutes, fifteen minutes — or how long? Of course, one of the guides for this is, how long would you like to wait while somebody else talks? That takes us back to the "I'm OK, You're OK" position, or "I care and you care." That's what "I'm OK, You're OK" means. I care about you, and I know you care about me. That's the basis for your contract. Now you'll make the length of time on the telephone balance with the amount of patience that each of you has and your special telephone needs. What do you think is fair? It depends on how many people there are in your family. If there are six or eight and everyone needs to use the telephone at some time during the evening, then maybe it has to be a shorter period. Sharing, according to each person's needs (Junior, age 4, doesn't need the telephone as much as Mom or you).

There's another thing to think about. Are you being fair to your friends if you are constantly making long telephone calls? If the telephone is always busy, there's no way for your other friends to reach you. And that's pretty important — that you are able to be reached as well as being able to reach other people. How much time should you leave open so that other people can call you? How many times a day or an evening can one person use the telephone? Then again, if you're having a long conversation, and someone else needs to use the telephone urgently, can you work out an agreement that says it's okay to interrupt you without your getting angry about it? Perhaps a signal to the user that they should end their conversation within thirty seconds or a minute would be helpful. This is to avoid being rude to the caller, of course, while at the same time letting your listerner know that someone else wants to use the phone. This is not a serious problem, and yet, I've heard lots of arguments about the telephone. In one home I know, a girl got in such a hassle over the length of time that she was using the telephone that Dad bought her her own telephone. Then that became a problem because whenever she would violate some other contract, such as coming home late, or not doing her homework, he would use the telephone as punishment. He'd say, "I'm going to have that telephone taken out." And, in fact, he did. This was an unhappy kind of relationship.

THE UNWRITTEN CONTRACT

One of the things that underlies contracts about telephones, cars, and the like, is an unwritten contract that you may want to think about and talk about with your folks. That is — to whom do the things in the house belong? So often, the old fashioned Parent tape is, "As long as you live in *my house*, you'll do things *my* way. I'm paying the bills, and it's my house. You're welcome to live in it, but according to my rules." This single tape leads to more kids leaving home early than any other. This, of course, discourages you from taking a real interest in making your home go and hastens the day when you want to "hit the road." Instead, perhaps, you could let Mother and Dad know that you do have an interest in the house working right. You can demonstrate this interest in a lot of ways — like doing tasks without being told, because it's "our" house, not because you *have* to do tasks which are given to you.

By the way you come on, you can begin to change attitudes in mothers and dads about the use of the telephone, and about a lot of other things. As Mom and Dad begin to see themselves as being important to you, as they realize that you are aware of their feelings, they will change. Very shortly, you'll find that things improve in a way you never believed possible. They'll begin to see *you* more as a PIC and treat you with more respect. This is one of the things that most teenagers are saying they want. They want to be

"Here's another thing to think about. How much time shou

considered as people and respected as such. Each of us wants to be respected as a person. Mothers and Dads also dislike being given the idiot treatment. We don't want to be treated like little kids, or bosses, or asses. I know that that is true, and you know it's true. Of course, one of the problems is for you to act in a responsible way so you'll be treated like a person of importance while still having little kid feelings and a large portion of limited knowledge. That "ain't easy," but that's what we're talking about.

WHO'S IN CHARGE HERE?

Another problem that makes it very difficult for teens is that many PIC's act like Kids. This is very confusing for anyone your age who wants to use older people as models. Maybe they'll be acting more in their Kid than you. You then find it difficult to pattern yourself after them. Another thing to keep in mind is that PIC are not always consistent. They don't always do or say the same thing or always mean what they say. Just like you. When one is angry, the Kid may do and say things that later embarrasses the Adult and for which the Parent comes on in a heavy way. That doesn't mean that elders don't have some good ideas and that because they goof they should be written off as total losses. No one is perfect. But, elders have one advantage — they've had more time to learn from their mistakes. You can make your own (and you will), but you don't have to repeat theirs.

So, using the telephone intelligently is a matter of acting in a more thoughtful way. Someone who makes sense and who cares about other people, is aware that other people have wants and needs. If you take care of the needs of others, you'll probably have more time on the telephone with less hassle.

"...ou leave open so that other people can call you?"

AWARENESS IS THE TA GAME

The way to use TA, then, is to become aware of the transactions and the games that are taking place. You know, when you damage the car, or talk back, or you're in a hassle with somebody, you may find that other people are playing "Now I've Got You, You Silly Old Person." (NIGYYSOP). "Now I've Got You," means "I've been saving this up for you. No. You may not use the telephone — not now nor any time. We'll just find out who is the boss around here." That's how the "Now I've Got You" game begins. All you did was ask to use the telephone, and you get clobbered, but you forget that maybe mother or father have been saving up unpleasant feelings (brown stamps), and have been putting up with rather unhappy things that had been going on, and they see their chance to get back at you. So getting back at you is one of the games.

Another game you may play is "Dog in the Manger" (DIM). That's where *you* can't use a thing and won't let anyone else use it. Like you have your own telephone, are not using it, and don't want anyone else to use it. You might think about that one in terms of all of your things . . . your clothing, your room, your car, etc. Whether you're playing the game of NIGYYSOP or DIM, when you won't share with the family, just to get personal satisfaction at the discomfort of someone else. Getting this satisfaction can be a crooked way of getting strokes. You know when you deny somebody something they want, it usually leads to a big fight. You can get a lot of strokes that way. Then, if you can get a "courtroom" kind of decision from Mother or Dad to prove you're right, you're getting a lot of strokes out of that game.

147

*"A problem that makes communication difficult for teens
is that many PIC's act like Kids."*

*"When playing "I win, you lose" the other person picks up a lot
of brown stamps, and you can expect to get clobbered shortly."*

GAMES AND BROWN STAMPS

Of course, you've got to remember that when you're playing an "I win,
you lose" game, the other guy is picking up a lot of brown stamps. You can
expect to get clobbered very shortly thereafter. You know, like later when
you want to borrow something, expect the other person not to give it to you,
and to deny it with a lot of satisfaction at putting you down. Well, that's the
problem with tough games. You get a lot of strokes at the time, but people
tend to get back at you. The reason we do this is that the Kid in us doesn't
really take account of what is going to happen. It's only concerned with
feeling good at the time. So if you want to get out of games, one of the first
steps is to *become aware of what is going on right now*. Am I playing a
game? Am I playing "Dog in the Manger" or "NIGYYSOP" or "I Want My
Way," or "If It Wasn't For You," or "Look What You Did to Me Now," etc.
If you're playing any of these games, or "Hey, Ma, Look What He's Doing"
(tattletale), or getting someone else into trouble, stop it! Just quit! Start
coming on straighter. Tell them what you want. Tell them in a straight
way, "I know you want the telephone, and it's okay." Limit it to three
minutes or five minutes or however long you want to limit it. But make your
contract, and have enough understanding to realize that there may be
times to be more lenient. That's the basis for getting along better. And,
also, if you're using the telephone and someone has indicated they need the
phone, make sure that you get off as quickly as possible. That means that
you're caring about them, and then they're not so unwilling to let you use it
next time.

Some of the same ideas apply to other things we'll talk about. Two rules for getting along:

1. Be kind.
2. Don't carry malice (hate). Get rid of it.
   Talk it out. But don't save it.

DOING DISHES

There's one I can talk about. I can remember in our house that my Mother and Dad were very kind. If the dishes needed doing, they went ahead and did them. I don't think that was right. I didn't think it was right or fair then, but I was so selfish then I just let them do it even though they were very tired, too. In our present house, when my sons were growing up and began doing their thing, both of them knew how to do the dishes. And, at first, they enjoyed showing us how well they could do it and how cooperative they were. After a while, when the tasks were repeated often enough, dishes got to be a drag. They decided they didn't want to do them, and I was saying I didn't want to do them. Their mother, being a very nice person, said she would do them. Of course, I realized that that wasn't being very fair, so we had a family conference. We had a contract making session in which each of us talked about the way we felt about doing dishes.

"A contract can be made about doing dishes."

The boys, basically, had a sense of fairness, of fair play, so they worked it out between them that the only dishes really to be concerned about were dinner dishes. For breakfast, we would each do our own. We agreed that as we left the table, we'd each take our dishes, rinse them off, and put them in the dishwasher. Then maybe Mother, or the last person, would put away things like butter and common dishes, etc. Of course, we all ate breakfast at different times, so that made it simpler to handle. At lunch, none of us were ever at home, and if we were, it wasn't a very big deal anyhow.

But dinner got to be a hassle. So the way we all worked it out was the boys would do the dishes on weekdays, since Marge and I both worked and I worked at night, very often. Since Marge did most of the work preparing the dinner, she shouldn't have to do dishes. And, since I worked both during the day and evening, it wasn't fair to have me do them during the week. So they would take turns doing the evening meal dishes. The way they decided to get out of the hassle over whose turn it was was settled by the suggestion that Monday, Wednesday and Friday would be Mark's days — the first letter of Mark's name was M so that would be easy to remember, and the other days would be Larry's — Tuesday, Thursday and Saturday. That left Sunday. They were quick to recognize that I didn't work on Sunday, so then it was my job on Sunday night to do the dishes. And, for the remaining time that the boys were in our home, that was the contract, and that's the way it worked. And, I confess, I used to fuss about doing mine on Sunday night. Of course, it was always in fun, and I would do the dishes. Also, we had a flexibility clause that if somebody had something to do that was pressing, they could trade off with someone else, and that worked out pretty well.

"OH! HOW I HATE TO GET UP IN THE MORNING."*

Another contract that we worked out very well was getting up in the morning. For years, the boys and I were difficult to wake up and get out of bed. We were grumpy, and Marge was very unhappy because she would get up early and then she would take the responsibility of seeing to it that we got up. So, by the time we were up and eating our breakfast, she was down, unhappy, and discouraged. We worked out a contract on that. She would wake us, but she would not be responsible for our getting up and getting on our way. A little later everyone had his own clock-radio and took complete responsiblity for waking and getting up. The perils that we faced if we didn't get up were to be the responsibility of the individual not meeting his obligations, whether it be to get to school or to get to work. And, surprisingly enough, all of our habits changed, and from then on, no one had any great difficulty getting up and getting on his way. The result of that, of course, was that it changed, for me, a lifetime habit to one where I began to take responsibility for myself. It also relieved Marge of the unpleasantness of having to deal with three grumpy guys in the morning.

I don't know that our family has been any more successful in working out our life problems, but these are some simple solutions that did work for us. Maybe you can use some of them to work out the things that are bugging you and the people you care about.

TAKING OUT THE GARBAGE

One of the more difficult things to work out is the task of taking out the rubbish. Almost weekly, a family in trouble will describe how their son "Will not do anything, like take out the rubbish."

Rubbish is a constant, recurrent problem — waste baskets get filled and rubbish boxes have to be emptied and the task is never a pleasant one. But,

*A World War I song by Irving Berlin. Ask your grandparents to sing it for you.

*"Almost weekly, parents describe how their son
"Will not do anything", like take out the garbage."*

traditionally, the boy in the family gets stuck with it. And, for some reason, there seems to be a masculine aspect to taking out garbage much like cooking or washing dishes is a feminine "chore." This is traditional. But, because it's traditional doesn't mean that's the way it has to be in your house. Chores are chores, and are neither male or female. So, working out a good contract about the rubbish, based on fairness, might be one approach. You can make agreements with people to take turns taking out the garbage, or to take it out maybe a week at a time. More than one person can be involved. Others, than "the youngest" member or "the boy," can take turns. Then nobody will feel he's stuck with a particularly odorous job.

Another way is to rotate jobs so that some days it's garbage day for you, and another time it's dishes, dusting, watering the lawn, cleaning the pool, etc. They're all tasks that go with having a neat, comfortable home where you live with your folks, brothers, sisters, grandmothers, and grandfathers. One of the country's modern philosophies is "to each his own." Sometimes people can't do things because of physical limitations. Naturally, you don't expect grandmother or grandfather to do heavy work. You don't expect a little brother, 4 years old, to do as much as you do. By the same token, maybe you can make it clear to all that you're playing fair. Then maybe the grownups in the family will feel more inclined to take part

152

of the responsibility when it is fair for them to do so. This won't always work. Grownups are not always fair. But, that doesn't mean that you can't make that effort, and by constantly talking about fair play and sportsmanship, you may appeal to an old Parent tape that runs pretty strong in most PIC heads, and they'll begin to get the message that they're not being fair when they stick you with meaningless tasks because you're young. That's one way of getting around it. To talk about fair play and sportsmanship and also fair contracts and getting a good shake for everybody.

I should keep my contract because I gave my word of honor.

I will do it because I said I would, and because it needs doing.

I don't want to do this because I <u>hate</u> contracts!

"Our Adult keeps contracts."

OF DATES AND TRUST AND WELCHERS

Now, if you go for that, if you go for being fair and you go for asking for a fair share of things like the use of the telephone, or sharing the tasks with other people (like taking out the garbage), *then you also are obligated to be fair about keeping the contracts that you make.* This is essential and takes practice. Our Adult keeps contracts and, whether this has to do with garbage or telephones or staying out late, it's necessary that, if you're going *to be trusted,* that you show you are *worthy of trust* by keeping your end of the bargains you make. And that's what this is all about. That takes some Adult.

Keeping a contract takes turning on your head (Adult) and making sure that you don't let your Kid get out of hand. Because your Kid doesn't like contracts. "I (C) like to have what I want, when I want it." Well it's all right to indulge your Kid and to make sure your Kid has a lot of fun, and gets a lot of strokes, and has good times. But at the same time, the Kid is pretty self-centered and self-concerned. The Child in us doesn't take into account other people's feelings nor the results of present behavior on future trust. The Kid in you will tend to make any kind of agreement to get what it wants. The Kid, if not controlled by a strong Adult and firm Parent, will welch on an agreement. (And, I'm sure that you don't like a welcher, nor want to be one). A welcher is somebody who makes an agreement (contract) and doesn't keep it. He lacks integrity (See Chapter 10). It's pretty hard to depend on a welcher, or to trust one. So, if you want to be somebody who is trusted, *live up to your contracts.* Be worthy of trust. That sounds preachy, but that's about the only way I can say it. *If you make a deal, keep it,* whether it's with your friend, your teacher, brother or sister or mother and dad.

"Take a look at some of your Parent tapes to help you decide."

This carries over to going out on dates, or staying out late. If you have an agreement with your Mother and Dad about going out, the best way to get more privileges is to keep the contract the way it is set up — if you say you are going out for the evening, and will be back at a certain time, make sure that you are there. Don't play a crooked game of, "Well, if it wasn't for," "It was all his fault," "The car broke down," or whatever. *Make sure you're back on time.* If the deal isn't satisfactory, and you have to leave when you're having fun, *leave,* then prepare for next time by telling them how much fun you had to give up, how you had to come home in the midst of things, and would it be possible to stay out later next time? But, don't take the matter in your hands and change the contract in mid-stream. The same

154

thing is true of laws. Don't break laws because you don't agree with them. Work to get them changed, recognizing that not everyone agrees with you So respect the opinions of those who disagree as well as those who support your ideas.

DO WHAT YOU SAY YOU'LL DO!

Another thing that will make for a better chance for getting more lenient rules is, if you do what you say you'll do. Sometimes, kids come to me and tell me that they say they are going to go out to a movie. Instead of going to the movie, they go to a "party," (alcohol and/or pot). At the party, they will be doing things they know their mother or dad wouldn't approve of, and which would upset the parents if they knew about it. They don't want to upset their mother or father, lose their trust, but they still want to have *"fun."* Now, that's a tough one, and one that you are probably wrestling with right now. I'm not sure that I have a good answer for that, except maybe you'll have to decide which is more important; being considered worthy of trust and having a warm, loving, intimate relationship with your mother and dad, or meeting your Kid's demands in a way that is probably illegal, could be immoral, and might be destructive for you and your family. So this is where your Adult must come in and make some decisions. I'm not sure that I can make those decisions for you, nor would I if I could. Because, only as you do, do you strengthen your Adult. The Adult gets strong by use, just like a muscle.

WHAT'S UP TOP!

You might also take a look at your Parent tape, and see what's going on up there; whether you've been given some tapes that will help you decide. One I had was, "Something that's not nice is never nice." "Something that's illegal is wrong." I try to be guided by these rules. What are yours? Check these out for yourself. You also might use guides based, again, on fair play. Is it fair to put yourself in jeopardy so that you have to be rescued by your Mother and Dad? Because, when you put yourself in a position where you get busted, they *have to* take care of you. Is that fair to them? You may say, "Well, they aren't fair to me." That's a crooked game. "Well, they did it, so I can do it to them," is an "I'll get back at you," or a NIGYYSOP. If that's what you have going, maybe you need to look at that one, because games are crooked and destructive to relationships and grow out of a need for strokes. When people need to do illegal, exciting things (drugs, alcohol, etc.) they are probably not getting enough positive strokes at home, at school, and at play. Are you? What can you do about it instead of getting busted?

KEEPING DATES AND BREAKING DATES

Sometime you may make a date. At the time you make it, it seems like a good idea — fun. Then later, you change your mind, or meet someone else you enjoy, or hear of a different thing you prefer to do, like a party, dance, or show you want to go to. What to do? Three selves (PAC) to the front. Child says, "Skip the date and go to the party." Parent says, if you make a promise you should keep it. "You made a promise." Adult says, "If I skip the date, he'll be unhappy and won't trust me, and I'm building a habit and reputation of being a phony. But gee! I *want* (C) to go to the party." Well, there you are. What are you going to do? Building character is like building muscles. The more you use them the stronger they get. If you're building rules to live by, the way to firm them up is to use them. Anybody can let themselves off the hook by saying, "Oh well, once won't hurt". But it weakens your principles. Do it enough and you won't have any when you need them. That way leads to mental and emotional confusion. Of course, rigid conformity to rules is dullsville. So you, as each of us, have a problem. Talking it over with others sometimes is helpful in establishing a set of rules you can live with and still be happy and fulfilled as a person.

QUESTIONS FOR YOUR ADULT

1. What is the biggest problem at your house? Talk about how you might use TA to solve it.
2. How do you handle using the telephone at home? Who takes out the garbage, does the cleaning, cooking, dishes, dusting, cleaning the pool, cutting the grass, and so on. How did you arrive at these agreements or rules? How do you feel about them? Fair? Ripped off? Guilty?
3. To whom do the things in your house belong? Whose house is it? Do you like your house? Why? How would you like to improve It? Who would you like to get along with better? From what you've learned so far what could you do to get along better with that person?
4. What is respect? Do you get any? From whom? Whom do you respect? Why?
5. Whom do you trust? Why? Why not? Can you change that? How?
6. Do you every play DIM or NIGYYSOP? With whom? What can you do instead? What are two rules to help?

EXERCISES

1. Practice making a contract either in school or at home. Plan to have a feed back meeting in one week to see how it works. Plan to change the contract till it works and everybody feels OK with it.
2. Make a list of the Hasseltimes at your home. Then have a family meeting to see what can be done about them. (Just be sure you're not a "Know-it-all" because you've learned about contracts.)
3. Learn the ten rules for making a contract. Practice making a contract in a group, then during the next week see if it works; plan to have a feedback meeting in one week. Make it something practical.

IDEAS AND WORDS TO LEARN MORE ABOUT

1. Hasseltimes
2. Don Ameche
3. Respect
4. DIM (Dog-in-the-Manger)
5. NIGYYSOP (Now I got you you silly old person)
6. Welcher

Chapter XIII

DECISIONS AND REVISIONS

*"To be energetic and firm when principle demands it
and tolerant in all else, is not easy."*   Mark Hopkins

When you were little, you made some important decisions which were meant to help you handle your life at that time. For instance, when you were about two or three years old, you may have gotten a lot of criticism from your family. In current slang they often "got on your case." You may have said to yourself, "I guess I'm really not OK. I thought I was OK, but since they tell me all the things that are wrong with me (like I don't eat right, drink right, clean myself right, walk, run, or jump like they want me to, learn as rapidly as they want me to) *I guess I'm not OK.* Everybody else knows how to do all these things, but I don't. So, I'm not OK, and they are OK." Now, that decision led you to take a position which probably has been influencing you, as well as a whole lot of us, for the rest of our lives. Do you remember? Did you do that? Because, when we say, "I'm not OK," we say it to ourselves. We think we musn't let anyone else know it.

*"When we say "I'm not OK", we say it to ourselves,
because we think we mustn't let anyone else know it."*

If they find out that we're not OK, they won't give us any strokes, and we need strokes to live.

The decision, "I'm not OK," leads us to play a lot of games, and we've talked about games elsewhere. A lot of the games that you're already familiar with are "Mine's better than yours," "Look what you got me into," "If it wasn't for you," "NIGYYSOP" and so on.

TIME FOR A CHANGE

There are decisions that we make early in our lives which we follow for a long, long time. We are sure that our present behavior is OK because that is what we decided when we were little.

It's right to stick by a decision. It's satisfying to you and others for you to make a decision and stick to it. However, when you find that you are wrong, when the decision that you've made earlier was based on not enough facts or when you've decided that the decision you made is causing you a great deal of trouble, it's time to let your Adult take another look at that decision, and perhaps, change it. You can then decide on a new course of action. This is especially true of those decisions you made early (two, three, or four) in life. Those decisions seem especially important to you because you've held them so long and they've kept you safe (even though miserable) up till now. Those decisions *were* very important. But maybe it's time for a change.

I remember saying to myself, at seven "Everything I love either dies or goes away, so I'll never be happy." I enjoyed being a tragic figure for a long time. I went around feeling unhappy and hopeless — doomed to be unhappy and very sorry for me. And, how brave I was to suffer and not show my feelings. No matter what would come up good, I wouldn't allow myself to really enjoy it because it would change soon anyhow, and I'd be hurt again. It was going to die or go away just like the little dog that I loved, the little girl that I liked, and the beloved nurse (who got married). Did you ever make a decision like that? Did you decide something when you were very young which you're still acting on? Sometimes, after a sad love affair, people make the decision to "never love anyone again," because they are hurting so much over the present loss.

CHILDLIKE "NEVERS" AND "ALWAYS"

One of the things that we often tend to do when we're in our Child (hurt feelings), is take a single instance and make a general rule out of it and then live by it. I once made a rule like that without knowing it. I met a man whom I didn't like. He was a braggart and a phony. He wore a black mustache. Many years afterward, I met another man with a black mustache, and I instantly disliked him. It wasn't until I started thinking about, "How come I dislike him?", that I realized that I was feeling all my anger at the first man and placing it on the second. When I caught on, I was able to like the second man because he truly was a fine person.

SELF-FULFILLING PROPHECIES

We make some very important decisions when we are young, and sometimes our elders help us to do it. Sometimes they may do it for us. They

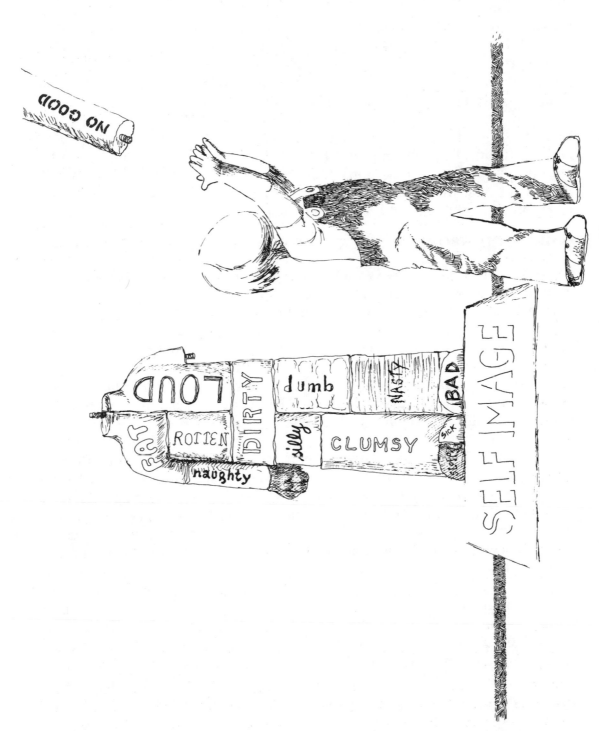

"Older people often give us information about out worthlessness, and sometimes we decide to be what they say we are."

may say, "When you're grownup you'll be a . . . ". Older people often give us information about our worthlessness, our laziness, our being no-good. They hope to change us by showing their lack of pleasure in us. Sometimes we decide to be what they say we are. Somewhere earlier I mentioned that Muriel James spoke of scripts. Scripts are a lifeplan or prediction that people make about you which you believe and then try to make it work. Dr's. Robert and Mary Goulding have a list of script statements which people are "told" in a variety of ways when very young, which they keep on trying to make work all their lives. Perhaps you'll recognize some of them. If so, you can decide whether you have to keep on making them work or if you can begin to write your own plan. Here's Dr. Goulding's list: Don't be; Don't be you (the sex you are); Don't be a child; Don't grow; Don't make it; Don't; Don't be important; Don't be close; Don't belong; Don't be well (or sane); Don't think (don't think about X (forbidden subject)); Don't think what you think, think what I think; Don't feel (don't feel mad, sad, glad, etc.); Don't feel what you feel, feel what I feel.

WHEN YOU GROW UP, YOU'RE GONNA BE A . . . . !

I know a fellow now who, when he was very, very young, was told by his mother that he was a bum. Over and over she insisted, "You're nothing but a little bum, right?" Eventually he was forced to agree that he was a bum. "I didn't feel like a bum, but I guess if Mother said I was a bum, I was a bum." Now he's in college being a "college bum" because he says he wants to stay there and make a career out of it. "Why bother? (I'm just a bum). Why get out and use my knowledge? I'll just stay here. It's kind of nice just living here at college, taking courses." Too bad, because he's probably a very bright guy who could do himself and the world a lot of good.

I know a child who, when she was four, said to herself, "I am not going to feel anything. I won't feel anger, nor fear, nor love, then *they* can't hurt me." Now, this sixteen or seventeen year old is having an awful time trying to feel what you and I feel — excitement, joy, and love, as well as fear, hurt or anger. Very frequently, in her effort not to feel, she escapes into a spaced-out place. (Do you ever do that?). Her mind wanders. She doesn't remember what you ask her, and so on. Well, she's becoming aware of this now, and she's attempting to get in touch with her feelings and to experience them. She realizes now that she's entitled to have feelings and to express them. She doesn't have to wall off her feelings, or escape from them, any longer. Best of all, she can have her fear, anger, hurt, survive it, and still be OK with herself and other people. When she does that she feels good, warm, happy, and alive. She has changed her decision and her point of view.

WHEN I GREW UP

Then there are people who made decisions early in their lives (2-5) about the kind of people they would be. One boy told me that his little sister died and his mother mourned for her so much that he resolved to make up to Mother for the loss of his sister. He decided that he would be the girl she had lost. Now, when he is in his teens, he's having trouble being the kind of

"Very frequently, in this girl's effort not to feel,
she escapes into a spaced out place."

man that his Dad and Mother want him to be. At first his mother thought it was "sweet", and she gave him lots of approval for this. Of course, he didn't get much approval from his Dad, and he's getting still less now from other fellows and girls of his own age.

Some people decide to be like their mother or father in order to be liked by them. Remember the guy who stole the cookies? Being like Mother and Father may mean *being fat like them, crazy like them, nervous like them, stooped over like them,* or a whole host of unnecessary or destructive things.

"WE'RE A FAT FAMILY"

Often, people come to me with weight problems. They tell me, "I've always been fat. It runs in our family." This, of course, is what they were told by their PIC's. "Oh well, Mother's fat, Daddy's fat, I guess I have to be fat. So I'll just eat as much as I want." They got lots of strokes for it, but it was based on wrong information. *They don't have to be fat. That's a fact.* There are other ways of handling this, but just dieting won't do it, so don't rush out grab the nearest handy-dandy crash or starvation diet. You could get sick.

Some unfortunate people have mothers and dads who do destructive things. Like they hurt others or themselves. In some cases, parents even kill themselves. The message then may be, "grow up and kill yourself like me." or "Grow up and do violent things like I do." "Be an alcoholic." "Go crazy." "Be nervous like me." No mother or father consciously and deliberately sets out to do this to their youngster, but mothers and fathers have a PAC and maybe their Child is "calling the shots."

What we're talking about here are messages which people accept as a way to live life. If you accepted them earlier you can change them now. Check into your early decisions, perhaps you can find how you may have conned yourself into becoming the kind of person that maybe you don't want to be. Your present actions may be the result of your early decision to try to please someone, or to get *back at someone.* If that's true, then you can change, now! You can now begin to replan your life, rather than follow the decision you made when you were two or three. It isn't too productive, now, to allow that youngster of two or three to decide how you should live your whole life. Often, men and women at 45 or 50 tell me, "I don't know how I ever allowed myself to get into this field of work. I don't like it. It's too late for me to change." (Not true!) They continue, "Why did I let a dumb 18-year old decide what I was going to do for the rest of my life?" Well, you may be allowing your dumb two or three year old (C) to decide what you're doing now. If that's true, and you don't like it, it's time for a new decision.

QUESTIONS FOR YOUR ADULT

1. What decisions did you make about yourself when you were very young? Do you still follow them? Do they work OK for you? If not, what can you do now?
2. Describe some script behavior you've seen in yourself or someone else.
3. What are some of the self-fulfilling prophecies you've heard?
4. You who are unhappy with your weight, or shape — do you think any of this is hereditary? Can you change it? How? Will you? When?

EXERCISES

1. Remember some of the "don't" messages you received when you were young. List the message. Who gave it to you? How did it make you feel? How can you counteract the message now?
2. Practice giving script messages to a friend and talk about how you both feel. Take turns. Then practice giving "living" messages to each other and discuss how that feels.

IDEAS AND WORDS TO LEARN MORE ABOUT

1. Self-fulfilling prophecies
2. Script statements
3. Hereditary, heredity

Chapter XIV

TO FEEL GOOD . . . WE THOUGHT

(Based on notes by Don Juhl and Charlene Kelly
of the
Aquarian Effort, Sacramento, California)

*"The souls of men of feeble purpose are the graveyards
of good intentions."   Author Unknown*

We all want to feel good. Regardless of our age, our race, our religious
beliefs, our sex, whether we are male or female, or the amount of money
we have. The one thing that each of us, you and I, have in common is the
desire to feel good. Our ways of feeling good are different because you and
I are different people. Sometimes you or I do things which may result in our
feeling good at the time but are destructive. The things we do may cause
changes in our bodies that can never be repaired or replaced. In other
words, *we can't go back and be the same again.* For example, for the
excitement, or because "everybody" in the group is doing it, or because
you're being challenged (Chicken!), you may have yourself tattooed. I've
rarely met anyone who, after having had a tattoo for several years didn't
wish to have nice, clear skin again. To get rid of a tattoo results in scarring
the skin. In the same way, the use of many drugs can make lasting and
irreversible scars on our nervous systems. The changes are permanent.
Tissue is destroyed and is not repairable.

I broke up with
Maria a year
ago!

I don't have this
"thing" about
butterflies anymore!

MARIA

*"Sometimes we do things which may feel good at the time but are destructive,
causing changes in our bodies that we can never repair."*

The topic of this chapter is the use and abuse of drugs. During the last thirty years an increasing number of people in the U. S. have been abusing themselves through the use of drugs.

I DON'T CARE, I LIKE IT!

No matter what parents and other PIC's say about it, young folks (and others) take drugs because they "like how it feels." They believe drugs make them feel good. Unfortunately drugs have become a dominant part of their lives in the teen years when their bodies are building and when stress is greatest.

THE DRUG GAME

Earlier in our book we talked about TA Games. Games are played to help us feel good at the time. They usually have destructive or tragic endings. Drugs have become a part of the Games we play, very much like the use of alcohol is part of an Alcoholic Game. You may not have heard of the Alcoholic Game. You may think of someone who drinks excessively as an alcoholic. In TA we think of the person who uses alcohol to his own destruction as being involved in an Alcoholic Game.

As you know it takes more than one person to play a TA Game and you may be that person. If you want to know more about that or you are involved with someone in your family who is an "alcoholic" and you want to help them or you get out of that Game, I suggest you read Dr. Claude Steiner's book called *Games Alcoholics Play: The Analysis of Life Scripts*, New York, Grove Press, 1971. But in any case keep in mind that whenever someone in your family is heavy into alcohol or drugs they are playing a Game and you are involved in it even if you are not the user. If you wish to break up the Game it will help you to know the role you are playing.

WHICH ROLE IS YOURS?

Sometimes you can break up the Game by not playing. For example, as you know from our earlier talks a Game is made up of three or more players; the Persecutor is someone who is constantly taking the role of the criticizer, the nagger, the punisher, the quoter of rules, and so on. The Rescuer is the one who does just what the name implies. He or she helps the Victim; advises, supports, acts like a Samaritan. In the Game of Alcoholic he may help the alcoholic person get sober. He may make them more comfortable, get them an ice bag, or headache tablet, clean them up, shower them, and so on. He even may get the victim some alcohol because the person feels so much in need of a "drink." In the Alcoholic Game the Victim is usually the person who uses the alcohol excessively. The only trouble is that usually at some point in a Game, there is a switch in roles. The Rescuer becomes the Victim, for example, when the alcoholic gets violent and beats up the Rescuer. Or, perhaps the Rescuer becomes the Persecutor and nags the alcoholic. So when you start out as Rescuer perhaps wanting to help an alcoholic, you may wind up a Victim with a black eye or broken jaw and wonder how that happened. Then you may cry out "I was only trying to help you" and that's a Game too. Or you may

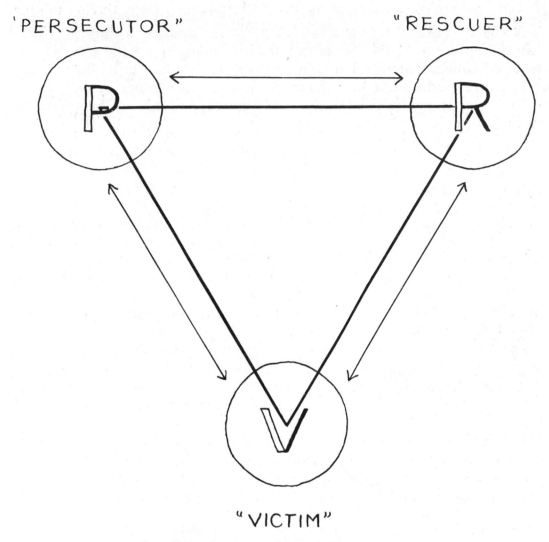

" VICTIM"

"The alcoholic/drug game is made up of three or more players."
Karpman Drama Triangle

become victimized when you help the person who promises never to do it again but does.

THE GAME'S THE SAME, ONLY THE "COIN" IS DIFFERENT

In the same way you can get into a hard drug Game. Drug Games are played with "kids" of all ages. The fact that most drugs are used illegally seems to make them more exciting, and excitement strokes the Child. When you are not feeling OK about yourself, you may be inclined to seek strokes that are illegal, because they are exciting and because they make you feel good. *When someone uses drugs the first time it's usually with other people.* By using them they get approval from the other users. They also are defying their PIC'S — it's like "us against them." So drug Games bring them attention and strokes they feel they must have. Sometimes they get positive strokes from people who are interested in drinking or using drugs. Sometimes drugs get them unpleasant attention from people who are against drug use, namely People-in-Charge, whether they are families, school authorities, or the law. But the drugs "make us feel good," they think. They pass them between each other and regardless of how destructive they are, they seem to persist in doing this with a feeling of loyal dedication. Recently, I'm happy to say, there seems to be less of this as kids are finding out that drugs burn out their minds (can't think, concentrate, remember, and so on). Many younger people are beginning to see that this crazy "in thing" is "out" just like "cool," "neat," and "tough" are no longer up to date slang.

"Research shows that the more alcohol a person drinks, the less control they have over their small muscles."

WHY DO WE SEEM TO WANT TO DESTROY OURSELVES?

Of course, drug use is not the only harmful habit. People who smoke cigarettes have been told frequently and officially that smoking is a cancer producer. The more we are told that smoking is destructive the more smoking takes place. I wonder if you have thought about that. We know that smoking causes cancer but smoking has increased, especially among people in the teen years. Have you given any thought to why this has happened? Is this a wish to get sick, an "I'll show them" kind of thing or what? I am puzzled about this. Maybe we feel that we have little else that's "ours" — that we have made drug use, smoking, and alcohol "our thing."

If we use drugs, alcohol and tobacco in a way that is destructive or irresponsible, we also play all the Not OK Games that seem to make their use reasonable. The truth about drug use is simple. *Most of us can't handle drugs like we think we can.* I am sure that you have heard of the drunk who says that he can drive better when he is drunk than sober. This just isn't true. And we can prove it. Research has shown that the more alcohol a person drinks the less control he has of his small muscles. We demonstrate this with the handwriting test. *After one drink a person's handwriting deteriorates. After two drinks even more, and after three, four and five the handwriting is barely legible.* And yet the person is saying that as far as he or she is concerned it looks the same as when they began to drink. Similarly you are not aware of the impact of drugs on your control system. You are not aware of how destructive it is for your awareness and how your ability to judge is being destroyed by the drug. We have no way of knowing what impact the drugs are having on us.

MOST OF US DON'T KNOW AS MUCH ABOUT DRUGS AS WE THINK WE DO.

There's a great deal to know. Oh, you know about reds, and uppers and downers, speed and hash, and so on. But most of us do not know why we use drugs. If I ask someone they say "Well, I like it." That is a pretty weak reason to destroy one's nervous system and one's life. So there must be some other reason. Understanding your transactions will give you knowledge as to why you are doing these things that are so destructive to you and other important people (OIP). One of the things that we do know is the OIP's can have a powerful effect on your thinking, feelings, and actions. You may think that you are showing independence by taking on drugs. But you are being conned. At first you're being led and later *pushed* into using drugs for the benefit of drug sellers. Then the drug becomes boss and your independence truly goes down the drain. The drug is boss and you're now dependent on it. You must work to support "the habit." So this is something to think about if you are looking for independence.

PEER INFLUENCE

There is nothing wrong with wanting to be like people in your group. *I guess what is destructive is when you feel that you have to be like the group for them to like you.* Becoming independent means deciding when you want to go along with the group and when you want to do your own

171

thing. Doing what you believe is right for you. One of the things that would be helpful when you are thinking about the use of drugs is to find out why you are using them, and the reasons behind the pressures and the cons that are being worked on you by people and groups of kids your own age. *How come these other people are so eager for you to use these things?* How come they say "Oh, come on, have a drink, have a smoke, here shoot up with this, or take a downer, it's great." How come these people are so eager for you to join them? Perhaps you might think about that. Is it because they like you? It doesn't turn out that way, really, when they ask you to rob or steal or get busted to support the habit that is developed. Maybe they don't care as much about *you* as what you can give *them*. Are you buying friendship at a very big price? Would you prefer to get friends in a different way?

"Are you buying friendship at a very big price?"

DECISION MAKING IS A SKILL

Making your own decisions takes practice. When you are facing pressure from groups and individuals your own age, it's hard to do this if you are under the influence of drugs. I have a tough enough time making decisions without all those chemicals that influence my nervous system and brain. I find it very difficult to solve the problems of living. I know it's more difficult to do it with drugs because the drugs tend to weaken my Adult and to contaminate it. That makes it difficult to operate. Drugs also knock out the Parent. Thus, we are left at the mercy of our unhappy Child which is at best an impulsive kind of Ego State and tends to do things which *feel good* but doesn't take account of what is going to happen.

HELP MOM! HELP DAD! PULLEEASE!

The interesting thing is that when you get into trouble through drugs or alcohol, you don't usually call upon the people for help who gave you these materials. You usually call for your family to rescue you. This is a cop-out (and a good one incidentally) because you have been defying them by secretly using and then when you get into trouble you yell to them for help. It's almost like you're blaming them for getting in trouble again. Maybe that's the payoff. To be rescued and get back at the family. Not much independence then, is there? What you are really seeking by trying to satisfy people your own age is pretty important to figure out if you are to achieve real independence.

MY ENVIRONMENT

If I want to know what makes me do the things I do, I have to take into account the things around me besides people. For example: the air I breathe, the books in my classroom, or in my room, the trees growing in the yard, the rain, the weather, the people I know. Things around me can make a big difference about how I think and feel and act. So if you want to understand yourself, it's good to explore and surround yourself with information about yourself and your environment. The places where you operate. If you want to improve the way you feel, perhaps knowing more about yourself and providing a happy environment is better for you. You may wind up in a more joyful situation than taking drugs usually provides.

PERCEPTION

One of the things that kids say to me about why they take drugs is that they want to heighten their awareness. They want to experience more; they want to get a new high. I often say to them "We can all get a natural high that is a lot more fun and a lot less dangerous." Perception is a word that means what we see, hear, touch, taste, and feel. How we contact all the things in our world. Our senses must be sharp if we are to be aware of what is going on around us and inside us. You reduce your ability to do this by taking drugs. Actually, what happens when you take drugs is that your ability to be aware of yourself is dulled, but the drug fools you. *You really close in your world and reduce your ability to experience anything*

173

"What happens when you take drugs is that you reduce your ability to experience anything but internal feelings, and these are distorted."

but internal feelings and these are distorted — like in a dream. But it seems so real. What's all this jazz about peers, environment, perception? What are you, a school teacher? I thought you were going to talk about drugs. Well, I am . . . but, you see, drugs don't have any brains, any personality. But you and I do. Drugs don't use us. We use them. So why we do this is important to think about if we are to figure out what's up in the drug use business.

For the person who only "tries" drugs, much of this is not important. Most people who "try" a drug like marijuana (pot, hash, etc.) are not hooked and they realize it's not for them. They usually use their ability to think for themselves and decide that bruising their brain isn't going to help them get through school or get the kind of job they want or the kind of life partner (wife or husband) they dream of. So they try it and don't buy it.

ANTIDEPENDENCE

For the person who depends on drugs to feel good, understanding one's self is essential if they are to achieve the independence they dream of having. You see, most of us go through four stages of development. First we are completely *dependent* on our family to survive. Then later we become *anti-dependent*. We feel we have to rebel in order to survive. If Mom says, "No!" we have to say, "Yes!" If Dad restricts us, we have to "sneak out" to show him we are independent. The funny thing about anti-dependence is that we are being dependent but in the opposite direction. We probably wouldn't do some of the nutty things we do if our PIC's hadn't told us not to do them. So maybe you who are dependent on drugs, need to look at your drug use to determine if you're using it to "get back" at Mom or Dad. Then think about who you are really hurting.

INDEPENDENCE

Another state is independence. Ah! to be free. For some, drugs (seemingly) free you to do and think what you want. Unfortunately this is an illusion, as anyone who is into drugs very far will tell you. You are dependent on drugs. That seems like two steps back.

INTERDEPENDENCE

The fourth state of development is *interdependence*. Here we can see people around us as friends . . . especially our folks . . . people to whom and from whom we can get love. Interdependence is not based on the all or none principle . . . you know . . . he never, she always . . . Interdependence deals with things right now . . . this incident . . . not all the time. Interdependence recognizes that Dad and Mother are people with strengths and weaknesses, good qualities and poor ones, and that each of us has a supply of each of these. We become less ready to condemn on a one hundred percent basis. NO GENERALIZATION ABOUT ANYONE IS TRUE. A person is neither good nor bad. He or she is a person. But when we are in the anti-dependence state we tend to feel not OK. We feel we can never be OK, or we can only be OK if we do everything or nothing "they" demand.

Kids!! Havin' problems wit' cher folks,
yer friends, yer teachers, the law?
Get a E-Z ta read manual here
what ONLY costs $5.95 plus tax!

"There is no book, no formula, no recipe for dealing correctly with people."

"OK"NESS, NOT DRUGS, IS THE ISSUE

Thus we may be using drugs because we feel Not OK and drugs are not the problem. Our tendency to *use them for the wrong reason* is the real problem. In other words we can't make ourselves feel good because we aren't OK with ourselves. When we take drugs nothing matters to us, even though really everything matters . . . matters so much that we don't allow ourselves to think about it . . . because we don't have an immediate answer. Unfortunately our drug use tends to foul up our thinking and this makes it more difficult to figure out ways of solving our life puzzles.

All of us have people problems. Solving these dilemmas will occupy us during our whole life. There are no right answers. *There is no book, no formula, no recipe for dealing correctly with people.* Thank goodness, too. If there was a right way and we used it, we'd by making "things" out of people. So what we need are tools . . . thinking tools to help us understand ourselves and others at the time things are happening. TA is one such tool and I happen to think one of the best and simplest to use.

SOLVING PEOPLE PROBLEMS

So all of us have people problems and usually people, not drugs, solve these problems. Answer the following questions and you'll be on the way to solving your dilemmas:
1. How do you feel right now?
2. What do you need to do to feel better?
3. How do you think you can do this?
4. How will you sabotage (keep yourself from doing it) yourself?

If your only answer was drug related, you're not dealing with your feelings in a productive way. The irresponsible use of drugs helps hide the pain of emptiness and hurt we feel in our lives. To use mind altering substances or not to do so is not a complicated question. When you decide to do so, you may be following an old decision you made a long time ago . . . I'm not OK . . . they're OK (HA) . . . meaning, "I'll show them how not OK I am . . . and then they'll be happy . . . when I kill myself." Dumb thinking, isn't it? I'm going to hurt myself to please somebody I think doesn't care about me. The one thing that people who use drugs have in common is their feeling of Not OK. Not OK is a decision you made when you were a little kid. By now you have enough independence to redecide . . . that you are OK and it's not necessary to kill yourself or poison yourself to get other people to love you. There are much better ways. Go with winners. Winners give and get strokes, they don't depend on drugs, on hurting others to feel good, or on hurting themselves to get rescued.

MOST PEOPLE DON'T ABUSE THEMSELVES WITH DRUGS.

Most people are not drug abusers. When you are around lots of people who *are* using drugs, you may get the impression that "everybody" uses drugs. Not true! Most people do not use and abuse drugs. Of course, most people use something from the drug store to help them get by an uncomfortable time . . . like aspirin or other medicine when they have a cold. Or even pain pills when they've had a painful experience at the dentist. But most people do not use drugs for fun . . . to feel good.

And not all people who do use drugs to feel good are totally lost and damned to hell. They may be pretty nice people who have gotten themselves into a jam and don't know how to get out. Here are some questions which you may have encountered in your life about handling drug related dilemmas. The answers here are not the only ones and may create other questions you'll want to talk over with your counselor or a "wise old person."

Folks always ask questions about drugs and drug abuse. We'll share the most common questions and the surprisingly simple answers:

Q. *How do I avoid getting into drugs and the drug scene?*

A *One simple way is to see it as "quick sand." You stay out of it by not playing with it or walking around in it.*

Our involvement with drugs should be seen as something demanding good information and careful decisions. To listen to those who "think" they know or to treat the subject carelessly is inviting bad results.

Q. *What do I do when approached to buy or use drugs?*

A. *Our ability to say "no" is super important to our being OK. If we can't feel good about turning down someone else's trip, we won't have a chance to feel good about our own.*

Q. *What do I do if I'm having problems with drugs?*

A. *Most folks who use drugs for a time have problems. Most of these folks* **can't** *get straightened out by themselves. Seek help from a drug or mental health program in your community. These programs will help you and keep your secret concerning your problems.*

Q. *How can we help friends that mis-use or abuse drugs?*

A. *Ask the person if they want help . . . if so, go with them or refer them to a "helping program" . . . if not, drop the subject and drop the friend after explaining why. Remember — you can't help someone who does not want help.*

Q. *What can you do about a friend that "deals drugs?"*

A. *This is a tough question that has three answers, none of them pleasant:*

1. *Ignore the problem and stay away from the action.*
2. *Warn the person of the results of their action and stay away from the action.*
3. *Tell the authorities.*

Q. How to get help for someone experiencing a bum trip?

A. Most communities have a drug program or a Mental Health Clinic. Call one or both and follow their instructions to the letter. If this is not possible take the person to the nearest hospital. If tthe person is not or nearly not conscious, call an ambulance immediately.

*There are lots of other questions about the do's and don'ts of drugs and drug abuse. If you are thinking clearly and OK with yourself you will seek the answers from the proper sources. Unfortunately, friends and/or drug users are **not** proper sources of information concerning drugs.*

EXERCISES

1. Make a list of sources of information and/or help in your community.
2. Role play in class: drug user talking to non-user about the "joys" of drugs. Try C-C and A-A transactions rather than P-C. Switch roles.
3. Do a research project, as a committee or group, on the most recent and authoritative study of the physical and psychological effects of drug abuse.
4. Write a description of some one you know who has abused drugs: his/her personality, hang-ups, P-A-C, life position.

IDEAS AND WORDS TO LEARN MORE ABOUT

1. Alcoholic Game
2. Persecutor
3. Victim
4. Rescuer
5. Karpman Triangle
5. Dependence
7. Anti-dependence
8. Interdependence

Chapter XV

DON'T LET SOME DUMB LITTLE KID RUIN THE REST OF YOUR LIFE

"He is wise that is wise to himself."   Euripedes

I often encounter people who tell me that they don't want to "do" what they are doing. I'm sure that you've encountered them. They say "I hate my job. I don't like being a mechanic or an upholsterer." Or others say, "I wish I could, (stop smoking, or overeating) but I have no "will power." Some make wishes. (C) "I wish I was stronger." "I wish I could get better grades." and so on. You now know where most of these complaints or wishes are coming from. The Kid, right? Most curious. They're doing things that they don't want to do, or not doing what they want to do. They seem to be in conflict with themselves. Could this be because they're listening to two different messages — "Be fat, be thin." "Drink, don't drink." "Live, don't live." "Be happy, be unhappy." "Like yourself, hate yourself, be guilty." If these fit for you, there's a way to solve your puzzles. Very often, we hear people say, "I wish I could get along better with people. I wish I was able to keep friends. Nobody likes me." That "nobody likes me" may have been a decision you made when you were a little kid. Maybe somebody told you, "Nobody will like you *IF* you do that." Then you decided, "I *do* do that, so I guess nobody will like me if they know I do that." Ever since, you've been going around making sure that people don't like you. And, if they happen to do so, you put it down as, "Well, they really

I hereby resolve never to smoke, drink, or overeat again.

HELP!!

I like to smoke, drink, and overeat!!

"People do things they don't want to do, or not do what they want to do because they're listening to two different messages. This is Double Contamination."

don't know me," or "They're pretty dumb," or "I sure fooled them." "If they did know me, they wouldn't like me. 'I'd better let them know who I am, and see if they still like me. I'll show them how mean I can be. That'll prove that nobody likes me, when they turn off." Did you ever do that? You want someone to like you so much, that you let them know how mean you are to see if they will still like you in spite of what you do, say, feel, and think. I have, and I hated myself in the process. I had the idea that nobody would like me, and I couldn't change. They would have to take me as I am or "tough for them." Now, that's the name of a game — "Take Me As I Am," or "Popeye" (I am what I am). A great out. I win both ways. I can be my own, rotten self and get strokes, or I can get rejected, play "Poor Me" and "See, nobody loves me."

FATE'S OUT — PLAN'S IN

Some decisions that I've encountered in people are frightening. Some of them are funny and others are sad. For instance, the decision to hate. "I hate anyone who . . . " So they go around looking for people to hate. Another one is the decision to die. "I'm going to die before I'm 25. I'm going to be like my father and not live very long." A young man of 15 had been carefully but unknowingly programmed not to live long because he was sick from birth and was expected to be helpless and die soon. Certainly he was not to live longer than his parents. So, when Dad became ill, he gave up. He stopped his therapy, stopped eating, and so on because he had been programmed to die before his folks did. Then we helped him change the decision, and he began to live again. Actually, his mother did such a great job of caring for him, that he had survived his original illness. He found he could change his point of view and survived the "don't live longer than us" message. He changed to "I'll LIVE till I die." He's doing great. It's like you cast a spell on yourself, that you're fated to die by a certain time. There's nothing that says you have to die when somebody else dies except you.

Is this glass
half full, or
half empty?

"You are nothing but a point of view."

Remember when I said earlier in the book, *you are nothing but a point of view*, and you can change your point of view if you choose to. *There are no spells*. No fate. There are no voodoos except those that we put on ourselves, or ones we allow (agree with them) someone to put on us. Then we obligingly let them influence us and the way we think. We don't have to do this. Keep reminding yourself that you don't have to do it. Do what you want instead. Decide what you're for, not what you dread or are against, and go for it.

SHE'S JUST A PICTURE, THAT GIRL

We tend to get all confused about who we are and how we got this way. Recently, a young lady came to my office saying she had made a childhood decision to "just be a picture on the wall." She said she didn't allow herself to have any feelings, that she felt all her family had wanted from her when she was a little girl was just to pretty and nice. They said, "She's just a picture, that girl. She's just so beautiful." So, she said to herself "Since my feelings don't count, the only way I can please people is just to be a picture. I'll dress up, be beautiful, and I won't feel. I won't be anything but a picture. Then they can't hurt me." And she went on being a picture with absolutely no feeling, no love, no warmth, and no fun, until she changed her point of view in a TA group.

Many of the decisions we make and the points of view we take are the result of what people tell us. People don't make our decisions. We pick up on the things that are said to or about us, and then act as if they were the truth.

THE CHOCOLATE COOKIE SYNDROME

Often, you may find yourself eating more than is good for you. Lots of people do. I frequently find fat people eating lots of cookies — especially chocolate cookies. They wonder why they are addicted to chocolate cookies, and why they love chocolate. I find, over and over, that people who've had a lot of exposure to their grandmothers (and grandmothers are wonderful people; loving and kind) eat a lot of cookies, and they get fat. Explain this? Are Grandmas who give kids cookies bad? No. Just the opposite. They give a little kid happy feelings. They feed them lovingly. Later on when junior feels unhappy, he eats cookies to get that "happy with Grandma" feeling back.

OF MARSHMALLOWS AND CHICKEN SOUP

Cultural things are going on here that I think you need to know about. In some cultures, mothers and grandmothers consider it healthy to be fat. So, when a little youngster is well-rounded from infancy, he receives the blessing of grandmother. "The little darling. Look how chubby she is. She's healthy, God love her." It isn't necessarily limited to any particular sect or religion or racial or national group, although some groups are accused of this. The typical "Jewish mother" is accused of overfeeding, especially with goodies and Chicken Soup.* TA talks a lot about marshmallow feeding

*Recent research supports Chicken Soup in treatment of cold, and other ailments.

and the typical Jewish mother who says, "Here, darling, eat this, it's good for you," while she ignores the youngster's feelings. And the child is saying, "But, mommy, I hurt." "Yes, dear, I know. Here, eat this. It's good for you. You're a darling, and you're beautiful." Thus she gives a sweet, airy nothing, (verbal ones also) which is known in TA terms as a "marshmallow." Marshmallows are shallow, sweet strokes to pacify but ignore, or discount child feelings. And, you don't like those sweet nothings. If you want to have your pain relieved, and they don't want to be bothered or don't know how to comfort you, they'll say, "Here, eat another marshmallow, and you'll feel better." You see what I mean? Did you ever get a marshmallow from somebody, when you really wanted comforting? Like, "Oh! That's not so bad. Don't worry about it. We love you, even though the rest of the world doesn't." That's a marshmallow. It really doesn't go anywhere. It doesn't go down either, especially if you're kind of sick to your stomach from all the bad strokes that you've been getting. What you want is some real warmth. OK? At any rate, there was a girl who decided to be like her mother. Mother didn't come on very warm; but, one *way to be liked by mother* was *to be like her.* Therefore, if she ate she got mother's approval.

*"Marshmallows are shallow, sweet, strokes to pacify
but ignore or discount childlike feelings."*

EATING FOR STROKES

So, two things. One is the mother syndrome that says, "Be like me, and I'll love you." The child echoed her by saying, "If I'm like her, perhaps she'll like me, and the only way I know is to eat a lot. That's the one thing she approves of." Another way this works is for grandmother to say, "Here, darling. Be good, sit down, and I'll give you a cookie." Bribery! That was one way for a boy I know to get good strokes. To sit down, be quiet, and eat cookies. As a result, he got to be very fat and very angry with himself and other people, including his mother and grandmother. Later in his life when he was angry and despairing he would steal chocolate cookies, even though he was on a diet. When we explored this with him, he began to realize that one way he had of getting back at "grandmother" (his wife as a substitute) was to steal her chocolate cookies when she wasn't around. "I will show *her*." When he discovered what he was doing he was able to stop eating the chocolate cookies. He also began to feel good about himself. He didn't have to get back at grandmother (wife, boss, etc.) by stealing cookies.

"When we're older and unhappy, we often reach for something to put in our mouths to get back the feeling of comfort we got when we were little."

The chocolate cookie syndrome hasn't been reported in the literature, but often, I find people eating chocolate cookies and other sweets that they first experienced with grandmother, who was being loving and kind and giving lots of good smiles and good strokes and, rewarding with a cookie or some goodies. Later they related to the good feelings gotten from grandmother and her cookies. So, when we're older and unhappy, we often reach for something to put in our mouths (cookies, cigarette, gum, candy) to get back the feeling of comfort and warmth we got from being loved by grandmother (or someone older and loving) when we were little. It isn't a bad thing to have a loving grandmother, by any means. Most grandmothers are loving people. They can enjoy you and love you and don't have to put up with all the annoying things that you do at home. They can just visit. When they get tired of you, they can send you home to Mother and Dad. Later on you try to get those same good feelings back by eating (and eating and eating).

If you are overeating, compulsively, and don't know why, you might take a look at whether you are feeling unhappy and trying to satisfy this unhappiness with food or other mouth things (soda, cigarettes, chewing gum, etc.) If so, you might find that there are other and better ways to solve your dilemmas than by punishing yourself, or keeping your anger in, and pushing it down with food, like you did with marshmallows, or by trying to get back feelings of contentment by eating something much in the way that you did when Grandmother was giving you lots of love.

I WANT A STROKE, JUST LIKE
THE STROKE I USED TO GET AT HOME

Perhaps the acceptance we get from friends when we use marijuana sprinkled cookies, or a cigarette, a downer, upper, and so on is related to our yearning for the early love and acceptance we used to get. Maybe the anger and rebellion, the running away, the striving for an early escape from home is not so much a rejection of home as a yearning for acceptance without evaluation, without being judged as "good" or "bad." Someone has said "a friend is someone who likes you." Maybe all that people are doing when they smoke or shoot up is seeking and getting satisfying, if only temporary, strokes from like-minded people. A healthier and safer way to get what you want is to ask for it. It's your right to ask, and ask and ask for *love* from your folks, you don't have to "sell your soul" to get it.

In your Child, there's a part of you which we call the Adaptive Child (AC). The Adaptive Child does what it thinks it has to do in order to get strokes. Your Adaptive Child gets strokes for what you do, not for being you.

The best kind of strokes are the freebies. The kind you get for being you. Some people feel so not OK that they think no one would ever give them any good strokes. They then decide to get strokes by doing destructive things. Many times, boys and girls conform to all the rules (goodie, pet, square, drip), in order to get strokes. They may turn out to be good students (greasy grinds). They study hard, do their homework, do their chores at home.

"Many times, people conform to all the rules in order to get strokes, and their classmates hate them."

They're so good, nice, and sweet, that PIC's give them lots of strokes. Their brothers and classmates hate them. In the past, brothers frequently hated their sisters because they were more adaptive to PIC. Many boys who strive for the male role rebel against authority. I'm not certain but I think there may be a rivalry for Dad's approval which girls sometimes get just because they are daughters. (Jan Fling says this is "sexist"). Some boys are adaptive and they learn how to please their folks and other people. They do everything that they're supposed to do and still are liked by their friends. Some turn into teacher's pet and mother's favorite, and so on. Other people aren't too happy with them, but they are getting all the approval of PIC's or "society" (all the grownups around). Teachers say about them: "I wish we had a classroom of kids like him/her. Teaching would be so easy." And, these "good guys" go merrily on their way, getting these secondary strokes. They don't necessarily feel good, but they feel safe. The Adaptive Child gets conditional strokes. In other words, "I'll like you on the condition that you do what I want."

I CAN'T PLEASE ANYONE

Adaptive kids are constantly adapting because they don't feel good enough to get freebies. Society and educators encourage this feeling by approving (grades, praise, etc.) only desirable behavior. Our whole society may be built around getting approval for doing things right. Maybe that's why we compete. But, that's another story, isn't it? At any rate, many times you may get the feeling that you're never going to do it right. "You never do anything right." Many of you have been told that. Or, you may get the feeling, "I can never do anything to please Mother or Dad, teachers, or anybody." In this case, you may then come to the decision, "Why should I even *try* to please them? No matter what I do, I can't please them, so I'll do what I want to do." Or, "I'm so mad with them, I'll just do the opposite to what they want" Well, then all heck breaks loose. Mothers and Dads get upset, teachers become frantic, and everybody is concerned. Meanwhile, you're sitting back saying, "You said I wasn't OK. Ha! Ha! I'll show you." This kind of behavior results from a strange trick that we play on ourselves. In the first place, you were agreeing. You were trying to adapt to what parents and teachers wanted. Now you rebel. You do an about face, and decide not to do *anything* they want. You feel like you're being independent.

WHO ARE YOU SNOWING?

If you'll think about it, when you're doing the opposite to what they want, you're really obeying them, but in the opposite direction. If somebody says, "Don't," and you "do," you may not have thought about it before, but you're doing it because they don't want you to. So, you're doing what you're doing because they told you something. That's independence? That's blind rebellion. Someone very wise once said, "A youngster is growing up when he or she is willing to do what he or she wants to do even though Mother and Dad are for it too." Doing what you don't want, just to

Don't do this to yourself!

I'm overreacting.

Nyah, nyah! Can't stop me!

"Doing what you don't want, just to "show them" may be destructive to you."

"show them" may be destructive to you. You may hate the results, and you may even hate doing it. So you may want to destroy yourself, or do something bad to you in order to get back at your Mother and Dad. That seems kind of dumb, doesn't it? Well, that's what a lot of people do. They overeat, overdrink, especially alcoholics or dopers who are trying to show Mother, "You can't stop me from killing myself." Well, you just found out something very, very new. A lot of people are killing themselves in a variety of ways in order to show PIC's that the PIC's can't stop them. People who are taking too many drugs, taking too much alcohol, oversmoking or overeating are usually doing it knowingly against PIC's approval. They're really doing a slow suicide in order to show the people who care about them that "they can't boss me around." So, if you are doing this, you may have to think about whether that is worth it to you. To live all of your life or to die to hurt someone or to prove something. I'm not quite sure what it is that you're proving, but one thing is certain, you're not making any sense.

I hear your Kid saying, "So what! Get off my case." Of course, behind this anger and resistance, you have a lot of hurt feelings. If you can begin to use TA to understand yourself, if you can get through the anger and the fear, then perhaps you can get to your hurt feelings and express them, and in that way, you can get them out and get rid of them and begin to live *your* life, not in rebellion, not to show somebody, but to achieve *your* wants and needs; to gain a real satisfaction and fulfillment in living from constructive behavior. To live your life in a truly independent and interdependent fashion, start deciding what you want to have, do and be for you, now, next week, next year, and in 10 years. Now is very important but now must also anticipate consequences (results) of present behavior in order to be safe.

BE AT PEACE WITH MYSELF, FIRST

I was rapping with a friend of mine whom I've known since he was a teenager. He had run away at 19. He came "out West" to find himself. He is now in his early 30's, and he said he had found that it is important to be at peace with himself before he can be at peace with others. This has been tragic for those who love him. I say tragic because his father, a very good friend of mine, died recently, and never had the opportunity to get as close to my friend, as I have. My friend is aware now of what was happening at his home. He picked up so much hurt that he had to mask his feelings behind his make-believe face. He put up a front of, "I don't care. I'll do it my way, and I'll show you. I want to leave home. I can't take this anymore." He was being very rebellious against the established family. Granted, that there was much to be said for his strong feelings. The tragic part of this story is that he went through 12 long years of searching for himself before he was able to come to grips with what was really bothering him, and to find peace of mind and contentment. All of this, perhaps, could have been prevented if he had been able, as you are, to take a good look at where he was coming from (P, A, C), how come he was so angry, and what he could do about it. These are things that can be worked out in a TA group, or with a skilled counselor of your own choosing. Trained counselors, especially TA counselors, don't tell you what to do, nor do they judge you. They teach you the tools that enable you to figure things out for yourself in a way that makes more sense, and which helps you to feel better about yourself and the people you love. In less than twelve years, too.

Now that John's described his problem, what do you think about it?

"TA teaches you the tools that enable you to figure things out for yourself."

IT TAKES COURAGE TO SEEK HELP!

An old "Parent tape" that often keeps people from seeking help from a counselor is that if you're a "man" you can solve your own problems. Only "weak sisters" need help in dealing with their private lives. This is as foolish as saying *anybody* can learn higher mathematics or physics without a teacher or books. Living, and problems of life, are not simple. That's why there are so many divorces, murders, robberies, wars, and so on. Simple answers for complicated problems don't work. So make use of people who have studied methods of solving life problems. You'll find your life becomes easier, happier, and more satisfying. Try it, you'll like it.

QUESTIONS FOR YOUR ADULT

1. What do you plan to do when you go to work? How did you decide this? Are you going to college? To take what? How did you decide? With whom did you consult? Have you "always wanted" to do this? Why?
2. Have you located any NOT OK's in you? What are they? Check them out with other people. Maybe they're not that bad.
3. Do you remember any decisions you made when you were very young? Are you still following them? Why?
4. Do you think you are under a spell? Can you break it? Do you think you are a WITCH? Why?
5. Talk about the "Way to be liked is to be like . . . ".
6. Do you eat when you are unhappy? Is there a better way to handle your feelings? Discuss the options you have.
7. Are you angry a lot? What about? Can you change? Want to?
8. Lots of kids want to run away from home. Do you? Do you plan to? Why? Where will you go? What will you do when you get there? How will this be better than it is at home?
9. Discuss the "chocolate cookie" syndrome.

EXERCISES

1. There are five reasons why some people have trouble at home and school. Many of us don't hear what is said (not listening); hear but don't understand the meaning of what is said to us; we mind-read other people (inaccurately), suspect people of things which aren't so and act as if they were; use past history upon which to base present behavior and decisions.

   Make up a short skit based on each of the above. Take roles to show how it works at your house or in school. Then switch roles and do it over again. For instance, John wants the car and Dad says no. John thinks it's because Dad doesn't like him. Somebody play Dad and John play himself. Then switch roles with John playing Dad. Everbody discuss it.

IDEAS AND WORDS TO LEARN MORE ABOUT

1. Marshmallow
2. Chicken soup
3. Chocolate cookie syndrome
4. Conditional Strokes
5. Voodoo
6. Witch
7. Role playing

Chapter XVI

SEXTEEN

If sensuality were happiness, beasts were happier than men;
but human felicity is lodged in the soul, not in the flesh."   *Seneca*

"Sex is one of the more difficult subjects for PIC's and teenagers to talk to each other about."

No book for you in your teens would even approach being helpful unless it attempted to deal with sex. This is one of the more difficult subjects for PIC's and teenagers to talk to each other about. But, sex plays such a tremendously important part in everyone's life, that it would be less than helpful to act as if it didn't exist.

SEX DRIVE STRONGEST NOW!

Statistics, as well as our own experience, tells us that during your teenage years, your sex drive is probably at its strongest. If you are not weighed down by inhibition and guilt, you are physically more potent (able to perform) sexually than at any other time in your whole life. Yet, there are so many blocks to your achieving sexual fulfillment during your teen years, that the conflict presents a tremendous problem to you and to your society. It's a problem to you because of your driving needs (C) versus your religious and moral beliefs (P). It's a problem to your society, which is encountering having to deal with the results of licentious (loose) behavior on the one hand, or neurotic (bad habits) or even psychotic (mentally ill) behavior stemming from internal guilt and conflict on the other. Part of your problem has to do with your own changing feelings — new stirrings in areas of your body you've been taught are private. In some cases you may have been told such areas are not nice, even bad and sinful. Dilemma exists in you about your feelings. The second is your relationship to others about these new sensual feelings. Unless you've been living in a cocoon or a vacuum you know by now about intercourse, male and female sensuality. Some of you are scared about this. You can't imagine yourself being attractive enough to be wanted (Not OK) by anyone, especially "one" that you like.

WHO ME?

If you've been doing a lot of self-discounting, you may believe that no one of the opposite sex who counts could like you. Sometimes people who are afraid of the opposite sex, or afraid of failure in sexual performance, or who have feelings of inadequate knowledge turn to their own sex for comfort. Then they face the dreaded world of homosexuality (fag, gay, queer). Recent studies indicate (Masters and Johnson)[24] that most adolescents experience a turn-on with some members of the same sex. Looking, touching, showing, trying, hugging, are not unusual and not harmful. What is harmful is the tremendous guilt and fear of permanent perversion if you enjoyed being touched by someone of your same sex. Not true. All of us can turn on if touched. We learn what to turn on to through experience, guidance, messages from PIC's, and so on. And best of all if you seem to be going in an uncomfortable direction for you, under guidance you can make a new choice.

ADOLESCENCE IS A NEW IDEA

Why are we having so much difficulty with this area now? You see, in the early years of this century, when young people reached their teen years, they began to leave school, perhaps in the sixth, seventh, or eighth grade. Certainly, very few went on to high school. They would "go to work" and become wage earners. Early marriages were the rule rather than the exception and led to comparatively large families. During that period, the concept or idea of adolescence, of being somewhere between a youngster and a grownup, didn't exist.

Adolescence is a modern idea. The idea of a "teenager" is a modern idea. Now, right now, if you are about 13 or more you have the ability to produce children. Amazing, but you usually aren't ready to be a father or mother at 13, 14, 15, or even 16. Right? You want and need more time, more schooling, more getting ready for a career, more time to play, or for adventure. The modern idea of extended schooling, of increased and extended dependency on grownups for food, housing, clothing, cars, doesn't usually take into account your need to express yourself sexually.

"In the early years of this century, the concept of a teenager did not exist."

So, this is a real dilemma. It's a real puzzle to you, and to your PICs who are concerned about you.

NOT TILL I GET MARRIED?

Surrounding this idea of extended education and delay of marriage is also the idea of "no sex till marriage." This rule is superimposed by church and "society" on your lusty, strong, healthy body. You are undoubtedly beginning to experience some of the frustration and conflict that this causes. You probably have heard ideas about being moral from your minister, preacher, priest, or rabbi. Ideas of cleanliness, righteousness, goodness, and so on. The same from your folks. You may have difficulty discussing your feelings with your PIC's because you thought that they all hold to the same position, in short that they will condemn you for having sexy feelings, yearnings and strivings. So, you kind of go underground with them and begin to consult each other, or maybe consult no one. In this case you may see yourself as bad, dirty, ugly, and guilty; or, defiant, angry, and lacking self-control. Especially if you are in a family or church that places high value on righteousness and abstinence of so-called "sinful thoughts." Self-hate and repugnance for yourself haunt you. Remember — you are OK!

GUILT

Recently, a young lady came to me for help. She brought with her a legacy of mistaken and distorted "religiosity." She came with a great deal of guilt about her very natural body feelings. She had recently engaged in some hugging, kissing, and petting (fondling). Her agony over this, her self-hate and shame, her fear that "God is leaving me" was tragic. So, this idea of how to handle one's sexual feelings in an era when there is confusion on all fronts, is not a simple one to talk about; not a simple one to clarify.

IF THERE'S NO RIGHT WAY, WHAT'S YOURS TO BE?

There are grownups, as you know, who adhere to the idea that sexual freedom should be extended to everyone. There are others who feel that this is weakening our whole national moral fiber. You read of sex in newspapers, you hear about it on the radio, you watch it on TV, in the movies. You hear a variety of ideas about freedom of sexual expression. No doubt some of you go to see pornography films. In spite of the ratings of motion pictures, which are supposed to limit the viewer I'm reasonably certain that some of you are getting to see "skin flicks." You may have enjoyed them, been stimulated or turned on by them, or frightened. This may cause you a great deal of distress, confusion, and feelings of guilt. It is with this that I'm concerned, not with whether you participate in sex or not. This is a personal decision for you. I am concerned with how you are handling your mixed-up feelings, with whom you're consulting about your guilt feelings, your feelings or urgency, your feelings of frustration and sex hunger, as well as your need for facts, for values, ideals, and guides for decision making.

SHOULD I OR SHOULDN'T I? PREMARITAL SEX.

This, of course, is the area that you are most concerned with. Very few of you are yet married, but you are concerned with the idea of whether it's "right," possible, or desirable to wait until you are married, to have sex. Yes, it is possible. Desirable? That's another story. Sex manuals vary all the way from suggesting complete abstinence until marriage, to recommending freedom of sexual exploration and experience in preparation for being a better husband or wife. I think that from a TA

"From a TA standpoint, your Adult must begin by
getting enough factual information about sex."

standpoint, your Adult must begin by getting enough factual information, to make the whole thing seem reasonable and feasible. People who are not married have the same drives as those who are. If you wish to follow your religious teachings, or those of your mother or father, then you may be confronted with some very uncomfortable feelings which must be handled in some way that is productive for you.

OOPS, I SLIPPED. NOW WHAT; DOES IT SHOW?

Then, there are those who are being sexually active, but are feeling guilty or fearful. An understanding of this from a TA standpoint might be useful. You have the drivings and yearnings of the Child (C). The Child loves strokes, loves to get close physically to others, as an infant or as a youngster. As one becomes an adolescent, this striving for closeness, for strokes, is heavily enhanced by the onsurge of pubescence and physical development. It's even stronger in those of you who have had feelings of rejection, of not being cared for or about by mothers and fathers or PIC's, of being overindulged (a form of rejection), or of being raised in an overly strict manner which discounted your feelings, may have decided you're not OK. Then you made a desperate change to "I can be OK and be loved if I perform well; if I'm good; if I get A's." Often, you found it difficult to produce good grades, talent, or superior athletic achevement. Frequently,

197

you may feel, "I can't do *anything* to please them." Then, you may get the feeling of being ripped off or short-changed on strokes. Thus, with the onset of your pubescence and physical growth, and an increase in physical growth, and an increase in physical strength and appearance, you begin to find that you're attracted to members of the opposite sex and they to you. Here, at last, is that long sought source of strokes. You begin to feel your own power, your own ability to survive without getting strokes from people at home and people in school. This then lays the groundwork for getting strokes from peers, from people your own age or older men or women. Some imagine that someone somewhere else will want me, won't demand conformity; so I'll work or drop out of school and run away. I encountered a girl from Texas today. She wanted me to visit her in her motel. She had come to Sacramento from Texas. She was pregnant, broke, and alone. She had run away. Now she was here, without friends or family. So she had run away. But her problems came with her.

Very frequently, you're willing to sacrifice the approval of your church, your grownups, or other people whose respect and love you want, for the immediately satisfying all-encompassing need for heartwarming and body-warming stroking.

I CAN'T LIVE WITHOUT HER/HIM!

Social relationships between people in their teens do not often lead to marriage, no matter how important it seems then. Very frequently boys and girls over-dramatize themselves, see themselves as heroes or heroines in the tragedies of ancient plays like Romeo and Juliet or West Side Story; conquering heroes. They visualize themselves as leaving home, being on their own, establishing their own families, doing what they want to do and coming home (occasionally) rich and successful. "I'll show 'em." This has led to the current fad of going steady where people dream of themselves as the same as married. Who needs that "piece of paper?" In this way, they deny and discount the need for marriage. In current vogue is the idea of living together to see if you *"can get along."* Unfortunately, and very often, the only basis for the relationship is the physical one. "I like her. She's fun," masks, "She feels good when I hold her." Often, as you become acquainted with your partner, you find that they do things that bug you, like he doesn't believe in brushing his teeth, or she doesn't believe in washing herself thoroughly.

WOW! I REALLY GOOFED. AM I A FALLEN PERSON?

Perhaps, he expects you to drop out of school and give up your plans for a college education, or he wants you to give up the career that you had decided upon. Perhaps you get pregnant, and this presents a very realistic fact — you now have to provide for yourself and a child, or arrange for an abortion. Old Parent tapes — "ought to marry" — make it even more uncomfortable. And, so, the whole thing becomes kind of a drag. If you marry, you find yourself having to do more housework, or more earning of living, and so on, than you had to do at home. You sort of yearn for the days when things were uncomplicated by the need of setting up a household.

> Know you just got home from work hon, but Mr. "G" wants me on the early shift so I gotta go! Meatloaf's in the oven, formula's on the stove. Could you call Mrs. Gidding's and tell her the rent will be late? And call the electric company too. We just got our third notice. Take the diapers in before it rains and don't forget the ones in the wash room. Watch out for the oil on the carport floor. It's dripping like crazy from your motorcycle. And I'll put the dishes away if you wash...

"If you marry, you may find yourself doing more housework, more earning a living, and so on."

I'LL PLAY IT COOL!

Then, there are those teenagers who decide, "I won't get involved in that scene. I'm too smart for that, so I'll play the field." So, they go about getting strokes in a sort of a promiscuous or catch-as-catch-can fashion. While this is kind of fun, exciting, and satisfying at times, usually it's frought with all sorts of discomforts, and even real dangers. In this modern day we still have the ancient venereal diseases which are, unfortunately, tougher to kill than ever. Even though they do yield to modern medicine, treatment is at best, kind of awkward and expensive. Untreated, they can be horrible. And, then, of course, there's the ever present possibility of pregnancy. We now have new abortion laws[25] and ways of handling unwanted children. These are more comfortable ways than we have had in the past, (illegal, clandestine, unlicensed operations) but it still is a frightening and uncomfortable, sometimes painful experience for a young lady to have, to say nothing of the fear and worry which the young man goes through when his "best friend" is in this kind of predicament. That's assuming that you decide not to have a baby. The complications and heartaches for you, mom and dad, and later the youngster, that grow out of having a baby and giving it away, I'll leave to your imagination. Then there are the complications of "getting married because you have to" (which is the silliest way I know of

199

establishing a family). *You do not have to.* I want to make that point clear. There is nothing that says you *have to get married if you are pregnant or if your girlfriend is.** I think pregnancy is a pretty poor excuse for getting married. It dooms not only you as a wife or husband to slavery to a child, but it also makes the child a sort of victim. He or she gets the feeling of never having been wanted. Being wanted is supposed to be essential to the security of the youngster.Thus, there is lots of guilt placed on the youngster over an unhappy marriage when he's told later, "If it weren't for you, we wouldn't have married." Very frequently, children of forced marriages are the victims of the marriage, and not its strengthening factor. So, the whole thing is a very complicated one, and it stems from the need for satisfying one's drives when it's difficult to do so.

WELL, WHAT CAN I DO THEN?

Self-caressing behavior has been labeled (ugh!) masturbation. It has traditionally been officially put down, but secretly practiced everywhere. I see and hear lots of folks cringe now when this matter is brought up, because it's such a personal matter, and even more, because of the many old, untrue myths that surround it — like it's evil, dirty, grows hair on your hands, you'll go crazy, you'll have morons for children, you'll get pimples on your face, and so on. All lies.

Self-satisfying caresses are not only harmless, they are desirable, satisfying, and safe. The fact that self-caressing is personal, makes it much more acceptable than illicit and loose behavior. There is no need to share this personal bit of knowledge about oneself with anyone. You don't usually share what you are doing when you go to the bathroom. We don't announce to the world that we're going off there to do whatever we're going to do. (Some people do, though and I often wonder why?)

Self-caressing behavior, which can lead to tension releasing orgasm or ejaculation, is a perfectly acceptable and delightful way of satisfying your drives without feeling trapped into a relationship with another person. Such entrapment can have dire consequences for you, and the other person.

From Masters and Johnson, whose recent research into human sexual behavior is probably the most complete that's ever been done, we receive the suggestion that self-comforting behavior has an additional value. It prepares one for becoming an effective love partner in pre-marital or marital relationships. Since each of us is unique, to learn how you can be pleasured can only be gained by you, from you. In other words, since each of us is just a little different from everyone else, you are the only one who knows where it feels good or where it's exciting to be touched on *your* body. Sex can only become a mutually delightful experience if each participant knows himself very well, and can guide the other person to how

---

*SB 394 (California) which became law on January 1, 1976, allows a girl under eighteen to buy contraceptives, and to receive hospital, medical, and surgical care for the prevention and treatment of pregnancy without parental consent.

he or she can be pleasured. Self-exploration and self-satisfaction can be very useful and is essential practice and preparation for heterosexual behavior. Certainly, the sensate focus (learning what feels good for yourself and partner) is the basis for modern corrective treatment in marital dysfunctions.

Of course, another reason for self-satisfying behavior being extremely desirable from a personal standpoint is that there is an unlimited and safe supply of it. Nor is it a substitute. It is a different and additional way of finding satisfaction in both individual and interpersonal relations. In the

"And this is my room. My brother & I share."   "What can she do all summer in France?!"

"I'll write you! And maybe you'll visit some day!"   "It's my folks! They're home early!"

"In the usual sex relationship between a male and female, there are many limiting factors."

usual sex relationship between a male and female, especially between people who are not married, there are many, many limiting factors. Place, time, opportunity, a desired partner, separations, shifts, vacations, family moves, present all sorts of complex problems. Self-comforting behavior by contrast is simple, easily accomplished, equally satisfying and available. As a matter of fact, those who have experienced both types of behavior find that the orgasm or ejaculation accomplished through a self-caressing technique is often stronger and more satisfying than that experienced in heterosexual ways. However, it isn't a matter of either this or that, because in marital relationships, both self-comforting and heterosexual behavior are equally desirable and useful.

KEEPING OR NOT KEEPING THE BABY

One of the more stressful decisions with which you may be faced, when and if you find yourself pregnant, is whether to have an abortion or to have a normal delivery, keep the child or to give it up for adoption. There are no "right" answers to these questions. Certainly, there are some people who are ready to settle down and to give up the rest of their youth to being a father/mother. This is not usual in today's world. There is still a great deal of necessary playing to be done. A great deal of traveling to be done. A great deal of education and growing needed to cope effectively with today's world. So, having a baby in these early years is frustrating at best and often wasteful of your human promise. In addition, babies are an economic burden to everyone, the kids, the families, the communities (medical, hospitals). In terms of the young man, taking on a wife and family, at a time when he is least able to do so in terms of earning a living and establishing independence from his own family, is difficult to live through and sometimes tragic. In no case, however, does there have to be the stressful situations that there were in the past best exemplified by Dreiser's[26] *American Tragedy*, where the young man, in order to avoid "disgrace," and to solve the problem, murdered his loved one. This is tragically unnecessary. The whole business can be less stressful with love and understanding between partners and parents. Happily, it is less stressful now.

But there are still families and small societal groups who set the stage for tragedy among their youngsters. If there can be mutual agreement on having the abortion, this can be easily worked through with a minimal amount of stress, minimal expense, and a minimal amount of risk to the temporary mother through community agencies. If, on the other hand, the young man has no further interest in the situation, and the young girl has to make her decision, this again is up to her and her family as to where they would like to be. If she has a tremendous *need*, and I emphasize the word *need* purposely, to have a baby, she should ask herself, "How come? What is there within me that will be satisfied by my having a baby." Perhaps, and this is very frequently so, you have felt not OK for most of your life — inadequate, unsatisfied, rejected, unhappy, put-down. Thus, you may be looking forward to a time when you can have a baby and give to the baby the things that you have felt shortchanged on. The false reasoning here is that you imagine that in providing your youngster with these goodies, you will make up to yourself for what you didn't get when you were a little kid. This doesn't happen and it's very disappointing, besides which, it's a much more complicated operation to try to raise a youngster than it is in trying to raise oneself. It presupposes that your life is over at 14, 15, or 16, and you will never be happy unless you live your life through

"I'M NO GOOD, BUT MY DAUGHTER WILL BE PERFECT!"

*"Sometimes a girl decides to have a baby so she can make up for herself
what she didn't get when she was a kid, through the baby."*

another individual. Of course, this is also a mistaken notion. The world is a large place. There are millions of people in it with whom you can find mutually satisfying relationships that will give you a greater feeling of adequacy in your teenage years than you ever thought of having when you were a very little girl or boy.

I can't find too much to support the idea of you, as a teenager, keeping a baby, since I think it's terribly limiting in terms of your fulfillment and especially in terms of the impact on the child of being blamed for existing, of feeling unwanted, of being unloved, and so on. If you have religious concerns relevant to having an abortion, then probably the best idea is to have the baby and to place it for adoption with some couple who are unable to have their own child and who would welcome it and cherish it. Otherwise, abortion early on is a recommended solution. A bill in California became law (SB394) on January 1, 1976 which allows a girl under 18 to buy contraceptives, and to receive hospital, medical, and surgical care for prevention and treatment of pregnancy without parental consent. For more information and help with this problem consult your "Planned Parenthood" organization, Aquarian Effort, VD

Clinic, or Mental Health Clinic and, if you feel OK about it, your own medical doctor, or heaven forbid, a competent psychologist or marriage counselor.

One authority in the field — Albert Ellis[27] — for example, encourages premarital sex, as he supports enthusiastically and humorously, self-caressing behavior.

Like your present writer, Ellis points out that most of us abstain from satisfying ourselves not because we don't want to but because we're afraid of what someone else will think. We ask, "Is this the *right* thing to do?" And then we follow with "Wouldn't it be awful if they knew?" Ellis points out that abstinence or indulgence should be based not on the ethical question, "Wouldn't it be awful if they knew," but rather on, "Does it harm any other human being, needlessly?" and "Does it harm me?" Obviously something as private as self-caressment harms no one else and certainly does nothing but good for you since it reduces your tensions in a totally delightful manner, is always available and in some ways improves you as a potential lover.

OH TO BE A TROBIAND ISLANDER

There is much to support this. Some primitive societies where sexual behavior is encouraged from infancy turn out to have very low, practically non-existent levels of emotional disability, or so-called mental illness. There are no large homicidal or suicidal statistics. There are no prison populations so common to our current, so-called "civilized" way of living. Most surprising is the fact that, where there is complete freedom of sexuality between teenagers, there is no premarital pregnancy. This is very surprising to most people. It boggles the mind a little bit, but the facts are somewhat supported in our own culture where married couples who are childless finally adopt a youngster and then, within months, the wife becomes pregnant. This may be after nine or ten years of sterile marriage. What this seems to indicate is that the way you think about pregnancy and babies affects the possibility of your becoming pregnant. Now, please don't go out and start messing around and say, "Dr. Freed said all I have to do is 'think sterile'." You're not a Trobriand Islander. Of course, in the current day, there is no need to run this risk of pregnancy. There are methods of contraception, including male and female contraceptives whether they be condoms, the Pill, or the diaphragm. There are also agencies to consult! (Planned Parenthood, VD Clinic, Mental Health Clinic.)

KNOW THYSELF

But, we still have this conflict between old traditional ideals, and the modern attitudes. You're lucky, in a way. You have much greater freedom to discuss, and to understand than your mother and father did. I might say, in passing, that one of the needs for PIC's who wish to have meaningful talks with sons or daughters is to achieve greater self-acceptance of their own sensual life. If you are to bring your wisdom into helping to solve some of these difficult problems you must deal with your own hangups, your own

204

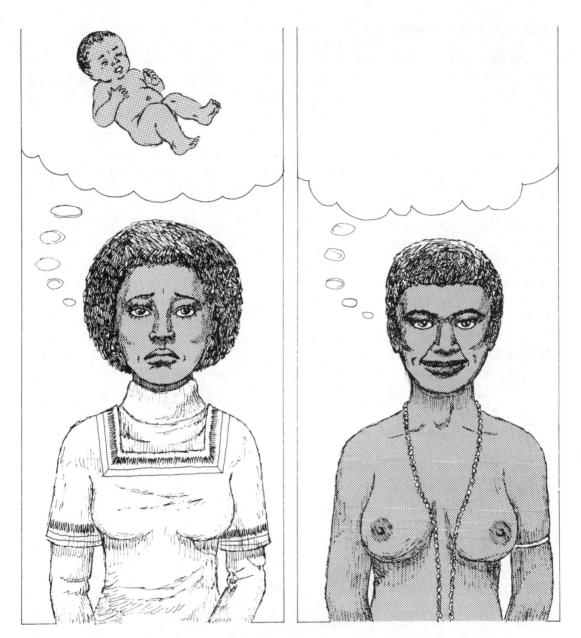

"What a comparison of certain cultures (such as between ours and
the Trobriand's) seems to indicate is, the way you think about pregnancy
and babies effects the possibility of your becoming pregnant."

feelings of guilt, sinfulness, and shame, and approach your own sexuality
in a much more open and approving way so that your own Nurturing
Parent can give approval to your own behavior. You will find it very
difficult to be open with Zeke or Josie if you view your own sexuality as
base, bad, dirty, or ugly. If you can view your own sexuality as something
natural and fulfilling, if you can approve and accept self-comforting
behavior for yourself as desirable, you'll have little difficulty talking with
your children about it.

I'M OUT ON A LIMB

I know, as I say this, the storm of reaction that I've elected to receive, but this is the way I perceive things. I don't feel that I'm alone in this, since psychology, psychiatry, and medicine have been saying this same thing for years. If you say it to young folks directly, as I'm saying it to you, you may set off a kind of an explosive reaction in some of the so-called "older generation." Accepting self-feelings is essential, not only in the sex department, but in handling your own anger, fear, and hurt. These feelings are natural and desirable and must be allowed to exist. We must find productive and healthful ways of expressing them if we are to avoid the tremendously destructive emotional traps into which we've placed ourselves. I think that, without handling these feelings in a more productive way, we are laying the groundwork for continuing and increasing amounts and degree of mental instability and psychosis. We must do better. Our old methods and values are destructive. So, whether we like this or not, whether there is agreement with traditional positions of righteousness, we have a very realistic problem: how to feel OK about ourselves while we begin to treat ourselves in ways that have been condemned by many of our civilization's most potent institutions, i.e. family, school, and church. I do not recommend revolution or revolt against such institutions. I do, however, suggest that, unless we radically revise our modes of "growing people," we will aggravate an already almost intolerable living condition.

So, there you are. Knowing about yourself is very important. Knowing eliminates fearing. But knowing doesn't mean promiscuity (doing it with anyone, anytime). Being a pushover for sex is the same as being a pushover or a patsy anywhere. If you give yourself freely to all comers, you begin to lose value to yourself, to feel cheap and worthless. You become a thing in your own eyes and in those of others.

PERMISSION TO ACHIEVE FULFILLMENT

One set of ideas which may help you is derived from a paper by James and Barbara Allen[28] called: *"Scripts: The Role of Permission."* The Allens' list, in stepwise fashion, notes the permissions each person needs to have to find meaning in life. Before one can solve the dilemma of "what am I here for," "where am I going," and, "what will make me happy," one needs permission to exist. Some people operate on I can only live and have meaning *"if* (I'm successful, have money, have a special person, etc)." *To be* must occur before one can experience one's own feelings and thoughts. To be a sexual being can only stem from feeling all of your sensations. To achieve lasting love one must learn how to care about oneself and understand the feelings of others. And most important, to find meaning in life one must have permission to succeed in sex and work and be able to acknowledge the reality of one's own feelings and those of others, and to place value on both. This is a far cry from promiscuity or even sensuality. Check yourself out against the table below. Where are you in your quest for meaning? Remember if you try to go from 1 to 8 without solving the in-between permissions you probably won't make it.

A PROGRESSION OF PERMISSIONS

1. Permission to exist.
2. Permission to experience one's own sensations, to think one's own thoughts and to feel one's own feelings, as opposed to what others may believe one should think or feel.
3. Permission to be one's self as an individual of appropriate age and sex, with potential for growth and development.
4. Permission to be emotionally close to others.
5. Permission to be aware of one's own basic existential position.
6. Permission to change this existential position.
7. Permission to succeed in sex and in work; that is, to be able to validate one's own sexuality and the sexuality of others, and to "make it."
8. Permission to find life meaningful.

"How do you handle the person who comes on too strong?"

HANDLING YOUR FEELINGS IN THE CLINCHES

What about the person that comes on too strong for you? Some people do come on pretty strong and too soon. Before you're ready. How can you handle the "all hands" boy who wants to touch too much, or the girl who wants to go further than you are ready for at the time? That is a tough question. People come up with this constantly. Should I or shouldn't I? Should I do everything that he or she wants me to do (that I want to do), even though it violates my morals or scares me? I guess one of the questions is not whether you should or shouldn't, but if you don't want to, how can you get out of it without hurting your friend. How can you handle it and still have a friend? One of the best ways is to stay in your Adult, but also be aware of the other person's Kid. When somebody is coming on pretty strong, they usually are coming on from their Kid. Their feelings are strong, their sex drives are strong, and they want satisfaction. They want to hold you, kiss you or hug you, and so on. If your Kid isn't ready for that or is scared because it is ready, your Adult can be your protector. You have some Parent tapes going which "know that isn't right," but that isn't going to cut much ice, because your own Kid may be saying a strong "Yes."

REMEMBER 4-5-6

You can use your Adult as a protector if you've got good material (facts) and have strengthened your Adult by use in the past. It's called building character. We mean having the strength to say No! when you know a thing is wrong and when you believe in doing right. You could give some good reasons if you've thought about them in advance. Be sure to be aware of the other person's feelings and tell him how he/she feels. This gets back to what we talked about much earlier in the book, remember? #4 — listen and learn; #5 — where am I?; #6 — speculate about him or her and paraphrase (tell them). Be aware of your own feelings. "I'm turned on, but I'm scared. I'm not ready for this, besides it's against my moral code." Be aware of your own feelings and your own values. Then turn your attention to where he or she is. Guess about the other's feelings. Then you can be straighter about saying what his/her feelings are and of where you are.

KEEP MOVING TOWARD THE LIGHT

Finding options for deep sex is sometimes a help. If you are in a tight spot in a dark place in a parked car, changing location is always a good idea; finding someplace else to go may sometimes relieve the situation. Talking about your relationship and its meaning is helpful. But, in most cases, giving lots of verbal strokes, and at the same time being straight about your own feelings, is very helpful. This is something to talk about, because there isn't any pat answer. There isn't any final answer. And certainly, there isn't any answer as to whether you should or shouldn't. The question is "What is it you want for you?" (and, which you, Parent, Adult or Child). That is something you need to talk about or kick around with people whom you care about, who you feel have good judgement, who care about you, and who are not wanting anything from you. One thing more. An excited "C" in another person will say or do anything to convince you to do what it wants. So the problem is whom can I trust? Certainly not your own Kid; your partner's? Not now, when we can't think!

WHOM CAN I TRUST?

Usually, when you have very personal feelings and are puzzled about them, you want to talk to someone, but you don't know who. So you play a little game of "What if." ("What if the kids find out, my Mom, Dad, my girl or boyfriend. Wouldn't that be awful")? So you keep quiet and suffer, or you "look it up" in a book — you listen to your special friend and find they don't know any more than you do. You think of asking Dad or Mom, but "they wouldn't understand." They might, but you're afraid they'd put you down or discount your concern. Counselors at school are trained to listen, understand and help. Also not to tell people and embarrass you. They can

"Sometime, if you have very personal feelings and are puzzled by them try asking a Counselor at school."

help in lots of ways you don't know about. Give 'em a try sometime on a small problem. If that works, you can then ask for help with more troublesome dilemmas. TA groups are good too. In group, members often feel better about themselves and each other and thus are freer to seek answers to their puzzles. At least there you'll probably get the straight answer, rather than a "don't worry about it" kind. Jan Fling, my "19 year old, going on 40" critic and friendly reviewer says she often talks to herself. She argues from both sides like the winning debater she is. She also talks to her journal or diary and finds this helps her tremendously. She says she can define what she means more easily when she can look at her own words. Best of all she likes being able to establish an "I can help myself, most of the time," attitude. Try it, maybe you'll like it.

QUESTIONS FOR YOUR ADULT

1. How do you feel about this chapter? Comfortable, embarrassed, outraged? Ask yourself where you are coming from (P-A-C) when you've decided on your answer.
2. Do you have a similar dilemmas to those described? What new ideas have you gotten from reading this chapter?
3. What do you think of Shakespeare's advice:
   Be not the first by whom the new is tried.
   Nor yet the last to lay the old aside.
   Does this apply to your ideas of morality?
4. Do you have all the information you need about your body? That of the opposite sex? Where can you get more? What books have you read? What books do your teachers, counselor, or folks recommend?
5. What are your options when you're scared about those strange, new feelings? Ask? Talk? Discuss? Act? With whom?
6. If you are a girl and become pregnant, what are your options (choices) about having the baby, keeping the baby, getting married? What are the father's choices?
7. What agencies in your community or nearby community are open to you for advice and help? Make a research project and share it with the class.
8. Obtain a taped copy of Albert Ellis' address to Sacramento State students titled, "Is there a Sexual Revolution?" Play it and have a discussion in class.

EXERCISES

1. Role play asking your mother or dad heavy questions about sex. Use an empty chair. Then after you've asked, move to the empty chair and give a variety of answers you might get! Do this several times till you feel comfortable asking. Remember use what, how why, when, where questions rather than . . . Do you think I should . . . questions that can be answered with a "yes" or "no."

IDEAS AND WORDS TO LEARN MORE ABOUT

1. Inhibition
2. Guilt
3. Morals
4. Licentious — look it up
5. Neurotic — substituting a "bad habit" like overeating to satisfy hurt, fear, or angry feelings.
6. Psychotic; mentally disturbed; confused
7. Intercourse
8. Sensuality
9. Inhibition
10. Adolescence
11. Virile
12. Potent
13. Repugnance
14. Abstinence
16. Pubescence
17. Conformity
18. Promiscuous
19. Venereal disease
20. Masturbation
21. Homosexual
22. Heterosexual

Chapter XVII

TO DO, TO HAVE AND TO BE

*"Ah, but a man's reach should exceed his grasp
or what's a heaven for."* Robert Browning

Most people who are 15 or 16 wonder what they are going to do for a living when they get out of school. Ten years earlier they were pretty sure what they were going to be. They were going to be firemen, a doctor or nurse, a football player, Olympic champion, an astronaut, or maybe a millionaire. It usually was something heroic or dramatic.

"Most people who are now 15 or 16 were pretty sure what they were going to do for a living ten years earlier, but are not sure now."

WHITHER GOEST THOU?

I really didn't think much about what I was going to do or be when I was in school. I was having too tough a time making it there at old Valley Forge Military Academy in Wayne, Pa. As I became older, though, and I got more information, I began to wonder, "What am I going to do when I get out of school?" Do you ever wonder about that? Maybe you and your family agree that you should go to college. Maybe you decide to get more information, more preparation, more training, more knowledge of a specific field that you're particularly interested in..

DOING WHAT COMES NATURALLY

Many people have natural skills. Some people are naturally good singers, or good dancers. Others are good mechanics. ("He's always been fixing things"). They seem to know how to do what others of us can't learn, even after much training. Do you think they learn a lot of it from the PIC's around them?

Perhaps they were encouraged to do these things when they were little. Some are good athletes, others good musicians. Some grasp math easily, others write well or can repair a car. Some can do many things very well. Some can't do anything well, but want to. Some are natural teachers. Perhaps, they've learned by watching their mothers, or dads who are teachers, or perhaps, they've had the opportunity to work with youngsters. Okay? Having such skills gives you clues about things you are able *to do*. The big question remains about what you want for you now and for the rest of your life. I know someone who recently got talked into entering an apprenticeship as a carpenter. The young man has great potential. He's bright, has an excellent memory; writes and sings well, is friendly and people like him. He is puzzled about making a living. Somebody said, "Well, with a basic skill trade like carpentry, you can always earn a living." So he tried it. With great energy. But a carpenter he is not. Also, he didn't figure out what he was going to earn, nor how long it would take to become a master carpenter. While the living would eventually be substantial, it wouldn't begin to meet his immediate or eventual wants. He has always delighted in good and expensive things. So, he began to realize that, while it might be reasonable to develop such a skill, it would take more years of training to develop into a master craftsman than he was willing to expend.

TAKING STOCK OF YOUR SKILLS

Perhaps you can take stock too. "What do you do well? What do you enjoy doing that you do well? Is it needed by lots of people? Can you turn that into a skilled profession?" Before we get to that, though, here is a suggestion that's written in the *"OK Street Fun Workbook"* by Dr. Whittaker. This probably was borrowed from Larry Mart's earlier work in which Larry suggested we make a Wants List.[29](See Diagram).

Make a list of your wants. Then in a separate column decide *"Where do I want to do it?"* Indoors or outdoors? In the country, or in the city? In a moving vehicle, on the ground, or on my feet? Behind a desk, a counter in a department store? Where do I want to do my thing? Where do I want to spend my 8 or 10 hours a day while I do my work? Am I content to be in an office? Do I want to work with many people, a few people, or work alone? These things can determine what you're going to do. If you like working with your body or your hands, there are jobs to be done. (masseuse, barber, dentist, and so on). Depends on how much time and effort you wish to put into the training. By and large use of hands and body, like mechanics, barbers, truck drivers (manual skills) pay less than those which require use of words and thought like banking, research, law, and the like.

At any rate, what do you want to do? List these things, not necessarily only in the vocational area either. "What do I want to do tonight? What do I want to do next weekend? What do I want to do on my next vacation? What do I want to do five years from now? What do I want to be doing most of my days and nights?"

WANTS LIST #1

WHAT DO I WANT TO DO NOW AND LATER

I WANT TO:	WHICH I? (P,A,C)	HOW CAN* I GO ABOUT IT?	(DATE) WHEN DO I START?	(DATE) WHEN WILL I DO IT?	WILL WHAT I LEARN MEET MY NEEDS? See #2
1. TO TEACH CHILDREN	P,A	1. Volunteer	This week	Now	No
		2. Take course in first aid or swimming, ARC.	call ARC (American Red Cross)	At end of course	No
		3. Babysit		Now	No
		4. Go to College, get degree	1978	1983	Perhaps
2. TAKE FLYING LESSONS	C	Save money, take lesson	6/76	12/76	Yes

*Think of short term, sampling methods to see if you like your want.

WHAT DO I WANT TO HAVE?

The second list is, "*What do I want to have?*" What do I want to have now? (Wow! I'd like to have a bicycle, or I'd like to have a car, or I'd like to have some new clothes or an airplane). Or, I'd like to have money in the bank, or a new wallet. List whatever you'd like to have. Let your dreams out, and then expand your thinking to, "What do I want to have by the time I'm 21, 31, 41," (assuming that, at age 15 or 18, you can imagine being older than 40). But, as one begins approaching a much older age, I can tell you that it really doesn't matter how old you are. Someone ten years older is much older than you. Someone said that the difference between boys and men is the price of their toys. What do you want to have now, and then? See if you can make a list of what you'd like to have for yourself in the next week, month or year, and then let your imagination go on and determine what you want to have 10 years from now. This might give you some guide on what you want to do.

WANTS LIST #2
WHAT DO I WANT TO HAVE NOW AND LATER

I WANT TO HAVE:	WHICH I? (P,A,C)	HOW TO GET IT	WHEN TO START	WHEN DO I GET IT?	WHAT WILL IT GET ME?
1. I WANT A MOTORCYCLE	C	Borrow Steal Trade up Save & Buy	Now 1976	Xmas 1976	Fun
2. A BOY/ GIRLFRIEND	C	Join Clubs Ask someone for a date Learn to dance, swim, etc.	June 1976	Sept 1976	Strokes
3. 1 MILLION DOLLARS	C,A	Pick industry where possible Get job Study economy Stock market Start at $1,000	After I finish school	By 40 years old	Everything I want

WHAT DO I WANT TO BE?

Then, finally, and these are related, "What do you want to be?" What kind of person do you want to be? Do you want to be like Dad or Mother? Or, perhaps you've taken some ideal person that you've encountered in a film or in a book? Some people only know what they don't want. What do you *want*? Do you want to be a doctor or a skier? Now, *doing* and *being* are two different things. You can do what a doctor does without being a doctor, like a nurse or a technician. Or, you could do the work of psychiatry without being a PhD psychologist, or an M.D. psychiatrist. There are psychiatric technicians or Licensed Vocational Nurses, or Registered Nurses (male and female) who work with, and help the mentally disabled, with limited training. Now we're asking, *what* do you want *to be*? If you *want* to be a psychiatrist, if you want to be a medical doctor, if you want to be a psychologist, or an engineer or an accountant, OK. It takes longer to get degrees. Usually pays off better, too. You can do bookkeeping without lengthy training, but to be the CPA (Certified Public Accountant) you have to do much more. You have to prepare for it, and pass certain courses and state examinations. Advanced work in college usually requires excellent work in high school. It's hard to keep that in mind when what you're doing now is no fun. But, what you are doing now is important for what you need to know now. It's also very important for what you're going to be doing at a later time in school. While it seems that school will never be over; while it seems, sometimes, that all this is just a waste of your time and effort, it is not necessarily so.

WANTS LIST #3

WHAT DO I WANT TO BE NOW AND LATER

I WANT TO BE	WHICH I?	HOW DO I DO IT?	WHEN DO I START?	WHEN WILL I ACHIEVE IT?	HOW WILL IT HELP ME?
1. A wife/ husband	P,C				
2. Doctor	A				
3. Motorcycle mechanic	A				
4. Lover	C				
5. Truck driver	A,C				
6. Bum	C				

* RECOGNITION:
Mr. Larry Mart, TA Teaching Member, in Sacramento, California, introduced the general idea of Wants Lists with similar headings.

WE NEED YOUR HELP NOT YOUR HATE.

The world has been going on long enough to have convinced many of us that doing the things that society asks you to do, in the long run, pays off in greater feelings of contentment and fulfillment in life; in living. I recognize that many of the things that society is telling you are sometimes disappointing. You sometimes feel ripped off. Sometimes have a feeling of being cheated. Recognize and accept that this is the situation in our civilization. But, to our knowledge it's the best civilization that has evolved, so far. The best that has been built, to date. It's greater than anything that we know of, and it's the best that we can do up till now. We welcome your help in improving it. We PIC's urge you to improve it. But, don't tear it down and destroy it without a proven, reliable, and safe replacement. One of the other things that I think it's important to remember is that, no matter what changes you make, it's going to be uncomfortable for someone. So, when you are thinking of changing things radically, keep in mind that you're going to cause a lot of people a lot of discomfort. You can minimize that by changing things gradually. Evolving things is better than revolving things (revolving things usually makes us dizzy). So, I would prefer that one of the things that you do is start an evolutionary (gradual) change rather than a revolutionary change. This will be something that you'll have to wrestle with as you begin to learn what you want to do, to be, and to have from now on.

"The second list is "What do I want to have?" Let your dreams out."

*"Whenever you're caught in a crowd, look for a different route than
the crowd is taking to go where you want to go."*

FIND A GREAT HUMAN NEED

One final word on doing, having, and being. I met a man on an airplane He was head of a large corporation which he had started himself. He was selling Vitamins. He was very successful. He told me something which might be as helpful to you as it was to me. He said, "If you wish to be a success, find a great human need and fill it in a different way." I've discovered that whenever I've been caught in a crowd, I look for a different route than the crowd is taking to go to where I want to go. I've found I get there more easily and a lot sooner. Try it next time you're stuck in traffic. Then think about it in terms of what you want to do, to be, and to have in your life.

QUESTIONS FOR YOUR ADULT

1. What did you want to be or do when you were 5 or 6? Do you remember? How about now? Any change? Why?
2. What do you do well (besides sleep and eat)? Do you like doing that? Why? Could you consider it for a job later?
3. What do you like to do for fun? Do you do it? As much as you want? Why not? What must you do to do what you want?
4. Are your goals based on what you want or what someone else says you should do? How do you feel about that?
5. What do you want to do, be, or have now? In ten years? Where do you want to do it?
6. What human needs do you know of? Which could you try to fill?

EXERCISES

1. Make up and fill in your Want Charts like those shown in this chapter. Compare it with other people's. Perhaps you'll get some good ideas from them. Don't be afraid to dream or change your goals.
2. Arrange to visit and interview people who are doing what you think you'd like. See if they're happy and contented. Why? Why not?
3. Visit an industry you know nothing about. Find out what kinds of jobs it entails.

IDEAS AND WORDS TO LEARN MORE ABOUT

1. Natural skills
2. Want Lists
3. Vocational jobs
4. Contentment
5. Success

Chapter XVIII

IN SPITE OF DEATH, DESERTION AND DIVORCE

"The relations of all living end in separation." *Mahabharata*

THE DEMONS OF ADOLESCENCE

Whenever someone suffers the loss of a loved person through death or separation, the immediate reaction is shocked denial. Someone says to you, "Did you hear that John's sister was killed?" You're shocked. "Oh! No!" is an expression of wanting to deny the unpleasant. It's as if you were to say, "I don't want to believe what I don't like." Very often visitors to my office

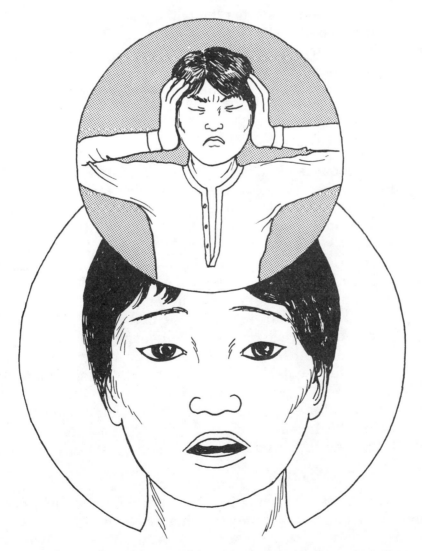

"Oh, No!" is an expression of wanting to deny the unpleasant."

223

express a similar reaction, but with a different feeling. Wives whose husbands died speak of them with anger. They are angry at him for having died. Usually they mask this with some degree of humor, like it was a good joke on them — the kind he always used to pull. "Leave it to him. He just *would* go away and leave me with this mess." Or, "Darn it. Why did he have to do it now? There were so many other, better times when he could have died than right now." Or, "Sure, he has it easy. I have to stay here and do all the dirty work," or, more sadly, "Maybe it was the only way he had to get away from me." So death, for the living is something to cope with. It leaves us with a mixture of feelings. Traditionally, of course, society expects us to mourn the loss of a loved one, of someone who was close to us. And we do regret their passing, if I may understate the case. In spite of all the anger and hurt we've suffered from our mothers and fathers, brother, sister, grandmother, and so on, when one of them dies, we experience a terrific sense of loss. And, along with this, sometimes we have overwhelming feelings of guilt. The other day a young lady was telling me that she used to get angry at her Daddy when he spanked her. She would go to her room and think terrible thoughts. She wished him dead, sick or some other unpleasant visitation, like "I wish his head would fall off." Sounds funny, but for a little girl it was a terrible wish. Then, later, her father did sicken with an incurable disease and finally died. Ever since, she has been carrying the feeling that maybe *she* was responsible for his getting sick and dying.

OF CURSES, WITCHCRAFT & VOODOO

Dr. Len Campos[30] has written a book tentatively titled, I believe, *Breaking the Family Curse* in which he talks about curses, witchcraft, and voodoo. He explains how we manage to enchant ourselves, to put others or ourselves into a spell by believing that what we *think* will affect *other* people, or what other people think about us will affect us. Now, this is not a put-down for the voodoo type of religions — the putting of pins into dolls and so on — because too frequently people have died from such treatment. But, it is probably explainable and understandable, when we talk in terms of Parent, Adult, and Child, to recognize that the Child in us has such limited amounts of information, such limited numbers of ways of doing things, that we're open to being scared. We're very vulnerable to the Parent-within-us (and outside us) which says "You shouldn't think such things. That's sinful! You'll be punished."

Some people feel that the person who died left them, and that therefore they don't count. "If I counted, if I had value to them, they would not have died." You see, it's that same old "Oh! No!" reaction.

DEATH A PART OF LIFE.

A most natural part of living is dying. We who are alive cling to life. Anything which denies us the idea of living, we deny. Anyone who dies, we may see as a denial of ourselves. So, when someone dies, we may say to ourselves, "Wow! If they can die, I can die, so I will deny them death and act as if they didn't die. They just went away." I would like to reinforce the idea that death is just as much a part of living as birth. Very few of us deny our own birth. By contrast, very few of us can visualize ourselves as being dead. This may account for why we take such unnecessary risks driving at high speeds, drinking or smoking, or eating (pills?) things which bring us closer and closer to self-destruction. We seem to have a fascination with death. We don't think it can happen to us. Maybe this accounts for our willingness to go to war.

"Very few of us can visualize ourselves as being dead."

225

MYTHS WE TELL OURSELVES ABOUT SUICIDE

Death is seen as a put-down. A denial. Perhaps it will help you to know that when someone dies, it usually is not their choice. When it is their choice, for example by suicide, they are telling themselves a number of stories or myths which are not true. Very frequently, someone who is contemplating suicide will say, "Well, *they* would be better off if *I* were dead." "They" means their loved ones. My usual answer to them is, "Have you asked *them* what *their* vote is?" I don't know of anyone who is contemplating suicide who would get a positive answer like, "Yes, go ahead," from someone who *cared* about them. But if they don't care about you, why do it? To please them? We may fun around at times and say, "Oh! Drop dead." Or, "Get lost," but even for our very worst enemies we very rarely wish them dead, let alone wishing death on someone who is a part of our family and who loves us very much.

Another fantasy that people give themselves when they are contemplating suicide is that it will solve all the problems of all the people around them, therefore, they will be doing everyone (C) a favor. Check that out with the people for whom you are going to do the favor. In every case that I've ever known, the bereaved says, with some degree of bitterness and humor, "Honey, if you thought you were doing me any favors, you really weren't. You know, you left me with a great many things that I don't know how to handle." It's the same reaction that mothers and fathers have towards youngsters or teenagers who take their own lives. I know of no mother or father who was pleased with the death of their youngster. If faced with a choice, all would willingly give their own lives to prevent their offspring from dying.

THE ONE AND ONLY PRINZ

Another story that suicide-bound people tell themselves is "I have nothing left to live for because I can't have this loved person." Underlying this is the mistaken notion that "this person only really knows and cares about me. Only he/she has the magic power to make my life worth living. The boy (girl) friend that I had, I lost, and, *therefore* I will never be happy again (because nobody else could ever love me so well). So, I might as well end it all." I never read Romeo and Juliet that I don't have the wish that they had stuck around long enough to find out what life was all about. Here is a fact. *There is more than one prinz in the world* with whom you can be very happy. And, here is another fact. The fun is in the finding and the living. So, when you are saying to yourself, "Life isn't worth living," I would like you to know that you haven't started living. You haven't had enough experiences to know where and who you are.

HAVE A HAVEN — GO WHERE THE STROKES ARE!

I hear your Child talking, Oh! Dr. Freed! You don't understand. He/she's so wonderful and I'm so blue! Sounds like an old song, doesn't it? Lots of feeling, but no facts. Your Child is usually entirely miserable, or entirely happy. Think of an infant when it's crying for a bottle. It's either going to starve to death right then, or it is full and contented. So the Child in us tends to get these desperate feelings. When that's true, your Child doesn't need to be killed. Your Child needs to be stroked. So when you're feeling unhappy, depressed, (futile anger) forlorn, and lonely, seek someone who will give you strokes. Go someplace where you're cared about, where you know people like you. Take those strokes and use them. Don't allow your Kid to walk around in self pity. Get yourself some good feelings, and then your feelings of desperation and desolateness will go away. One good idea is always to know someone who likes you, where you can get good strokes.

One of the more futile ideas about suicide is "They'll be sorry after I'm gone, and they'll give me the strokes they didn't give me when I was here." In Tom Sawyer fashion, we delude ourselves with the following line, "and, *I'll be around to know it.*" Now, there is an unalterable fact about death, and that is that *you will not be around*, and you will not know it. So, even if people do regret your dying, and do feel sorry for your having passed on, you will not be around to derive any satisfaction from their sorrow.

And of course since they love you (and they do) they will be terribly hurt. If they don't love you that's unpleasant but not fatal. Find someone who does and get strokes from them.

NO SOLUTION IN SUICIDE

One of the things that I know to be true is that, suicide will solve no problems for you who are reading this book. Ever. If you ever get to the point of wanting to take your own life, or even of making the effort in a playful way, please get in touch with someone who cares for you. Everyone of you has someone who cares, even though you may not like them, or you may not think that they know very much. But, each of you has someone who cares about you. I would prefer you to pick someone who is a professional like a psychologist, a counselor, a teacher, a principal, your doctor, your mother or father. Get in touch with them. But, don't under any circumstances, and hear me say this, *don't take your own life.* There are so many better things to do. So many other, better solutions. You know, you haven't been to the Trobiand Islands yet. You don't know what's there, or who is living there who would think you are great. Maybe you haven't been anywhere other than in your own home town. There's a whole world waiting for you. Not that that's a great solution, to run away from home because you do take you and your problems with you. So, whenever you're feeling desperate, I would like you to plan to talk to someone about other choices and ideas for solving the dilemmas of your life, get other options than the one you're presently thinking about. Other heads have ideas you and your Kid haven't thought of. Give them a try and don't give up on you.

YOU AIN'T ALONE IN FEELING PUZZLED

One thing you'll find out is that all the rest of us feel puzzled and desperate, too. But we figure out better ways to solve our problems than by knocking ourselves off. In line with what I've just said, in most of our cities now, there are Suicide Prevention Clinics and Crisis Hot lines. You can look them up in the telephone book. There's always going to be somebody

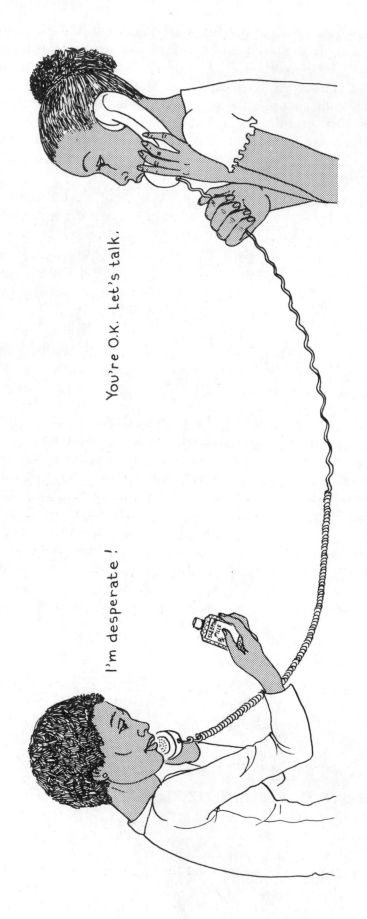

You're O.K. Let's talk.

I'm desperate!

"If you ever get to the point of wanting to take your life,
get in touch with someone who cares for you."

who will talk to you so that you don't feel alone. And they do care or they wouldn't be there waiting for your call. I've heard it said that suicide is the angriest act known. You might begin to think about who you're angry at when you're thinking of killing yourself and decide not to kill yourself to please someone you're so angry at. There are better ways to get it out and feel great.

DIVORCE

Frequently, people say to me, "Dr. Freed, you've written two wonderful books, *TA for Tots* and *TA for Kids,* but in them you sound as if everyone has a nice mother and father around. You seem to be unaware that there are those of us who are growing up without a father or a mother." It isn't true that I'm not aware of it. Certainly, I'm greatly concerned about it. I spend a great deal of my waking days dealing with mothers and fathers who are thinking about splitting up, thinking about getting a divorce, and helping them to solve some of their dilemmas so that they continue to live together in happiness and in fulfillment. And, I might say, as an aside, that one of the reasons that mothers and fathers frequently stay together is out of concern for the effect that their splitting will have on you.

Very often children wish their mothers and fathers *would* split up because so much hassling goes on around the house that it's a very uncomfortable and unhappy place to live. One of the things that I do know is that children tend to take sides. They think that if Dad, for instance, would just leave, that that would solve all the problems of the house. You may be thinking, "Golly! If I could just get rid of my brother or sister, wouldn't it be neat. Then everything would be fine." Blaming one person for everyone's problem is called "Scape Goating." Unfortunately, "Scape Goating" doesn't work because, you see, when somebody in a house is catching all the blame, other people are playing a TA Game of "If It Wasn't For Him." Games are phony ways of getting strokes, of not facing truth. We talked about that earlier. Games do not lead to contentment and happiness but to more and more brown stamps (unhappy feelings) and finally to more fights and unhappiness.

YOU ARE NOT BEING DIVORCED

But, let's assume for one reason or another your parents have separated. Dad left because he felt he'd be happier away than living with mother; or mother left because she was tired of living with him. She feels she would be happier away than staying at home. You're left with the other parent. Very often, you may think to yourself, "You know, I can't be worth very much, because Dad/Mom left me. He/she just packed up and left. He didn't care anything about me or he/she wouldn't have done it." Have you ever thought that? If you have, you might turn your attention to TA a little bit and see if you can figure out who's talking. See if you can find out whether maybe the Kid in you isn't playing a game of "Poor Me" (Little Match Girl) to explain away something that you don't want to accept. The facts are, probably, that Mother and Dad have some Games going that make them very unhappy. And, the facts are that you may be playing a part in these Games. In any case, you're taking responsibility for their breaking up, feeling guilty. Maybe you're just playing, "If it wasn't for him/her (I wouldn't be unhappy)." So you might take a look at the kind of Games you're playing when you're thinking about Mother and Dad having a divorce and what you are getting by playing.

Of course, sometimes a dad or mother leaves because he or she doesn't like you and there's not much you can do about that. But, for sure one thing which won't help is to stay angry. If you've tried to get the person to like you or become interested in the family again, and it hasn't worked after a few tries, it's best just to forget about the whole thing . . . and try to find others . . . people . . . who do care about you. Just because one or both parents do not care for you doesn't mean no one ever will.

"One way to handle the divorce of your parents is to follow the line "I didn't lose a parent, I gained a second home."

TWO FOR ONE

One way to handle and enjoy a divorce of your parents is to follow the line, "I didn't lose a father, I gained a second home." If Dad marries again, usually he'll pick out somebody pretty nice, different maybe, but nice to him. So you get to go and be a guest in their new place. Then when they start boring you, you can pack up and head for Mom's home. Mother will probably be glad to see you. In any case give up the idea that the parent who departed left you and therefore you don't count. You're being angry makes marriage splitting very painful. I've just come across a very helpful book which talks about how to handle your feelings when Mom and Dad split. It's by Richard A. Gardner, M.D., The title is: *The Boys & Girls Book About Divorce,* published by Bantam Books and sells for $1.25. Very good!

DESERTION

I knew some kids at age 2, 3, and 5 who were deserted by their folks. They were left alone, uncared for during three long, painful days, in an empty apartment. They became dehydrated (no water) and almost died before a neighbor found them. Later when they were restored to health and placed in foster homes they vowed never to trust any PIC's again. They said to themselves "All PIC's are alike — if you depend on them they'll let you down." So they went through foster home after foster home, school after school, juvie after juvie. They were determined to *get back* at all PIC's. This was the decision their Child made, and the pact they made with each other. I know that it was their Kid decision because they put everybody in the same box as their parents.

THE KID IN US IS ALWAYS . . .

The Kid in us figures like a baby — all or none, feast or starve, die or live, trust everyone or no one. In other words, the Kid deals in absolutes — always, never, everybody, nobody — the Kid doesn't see that *each person* is one of a kind (unique) and that each of us is different. Therefore, if you want to reduce your discounted feelings and live a happier life recognize that your parents' failures in duty to you are no failure of yours. (You goofed only in picking the wrong family to get born into). But what *you* do with *your* life *is* your responsibility. You can do better. You can make wiser choices of people to love and live with and achieve a productive, happy existence. It would have been nice if your parents had been responsible, kind, loving, and fun. But because they weren't doesn't mean you are not OK. You are OK. You can be whatever you choose to be. You have real worth as a human being because you exist. You are important to those around you. And you can think and act and love. So stop wallowing in hate and self pity and get on with your life. You're OK.

DON'T DISCOUNT YOURSELF — YOU'RE OK!

In any one of the 3 Ds — Death, Desertion, or Divorce, you had the opportunity to feel devalued — to feel you didn't count. On the other hand through TA you have the opportunity to look at your folks now as people with troubles. Thus you can begin to understand that they were neither

*"Stop wallowing in hate and self pity and
get on with your life. You're OK!"*

angels nor devils but simply people with puzzles of living. What they did, right or wrong, was *their* problem — they probably did the best they could with the feelings and training they had. Perhaps you who know about TA can do better with your life; maybe you can be more thoughtful of your loved ones, even now. Maybe later you will be able to pick out a mate who has a better balance between Adult, Parent, and Child so that there is more responsibility evidenced when you have children, more good judgement in meeting life's dilemmas and more fun and love to make your home a great place for kids to be while growing up and for you a fulfilling place to spend your life. I sure hope so!

QUESTIONS FOR YOUR ADULT

1. Have you lost someone through death? A long time ago? How have you handled it? Talked about it? Cried? Bottled it up? Denied it? Have you truly buried them? It's important that you do. Talk about it with your counselor if you still haven't finished with them.
2. Death leads to feelings of loss. Each of us is entitled to mourn for a while. But not too long or we may be mourning for ourselves. Talk about this idea.
3. Guilt feelings are tough to live with. Talk about yours with wise people. Maybe they'll figure a way to help you get rid of yours.
4. Does death fascinate you? Why?
5. Can you imagine your own death? How, when, why? How old will you be? Why do you say that? Discuss in class.
6. What problems has divorce caused in your life, your home? What can you do about this?
7. Are you angry at your father/mother for splitting? How can you get to feel better?
8. Do you blame somebody for deserting you? Feel guilty? How can you feel better?
9. Have you ever thought of suicide? Tried it? Why did you change your mind?

EXERCISES

1. Do a study on voodoo and other religions to see how they handle death.

IDEAS AND WORDS TO LEARN MORE ABOUT

1. Death
2. Mourning
3. Suicide
4. Suicide Prevention Clinics
5. Crisis Hot Lines
6. Divorce
7. Desertion

PERMISSION GRANTED

you
have permission
to
feel your feelings,
think your thoughts,
do
your act,
learn
your facts,
to
be free
and true
to
you.

REFERENCE LIST*

1. Freed, Alvyn M. *TA for Tots (and Other Prinzes)*. Sacramento: Jalmar Press, 1973.
2. Berne, Eric. *Games People Play*. New York: Grove Press, Inc., 1964.
3. Dusay, John. Egograms and the Constancy Hypothesis. *Transactional Analysis Journal*. 1972, 23, 37-41.
4. Harris, Thomas A. *I'm OK, You're OK. A Practical Guide to Transactional Analysis*. New York: Harper & Row, 1969.
5. Pemberton, W. H. Talk Patterns of People in Crisis. *Personnel Administration*. 1969, Mar-April, 36-40.
6. Gordon, Thomas. *Parent Effectiveness Training*. New York: Van Rees Press, 1970.
7. Berne, Eric. *What Do You Say After You Say Hello?* New York: Grove Press, 1970.
8. Steiner, Claude. *TA Made Simple*. Berkeley: Privately published, 1971. 1972.
9. James, Muriel & Jongeward, Dorothy. *Born to Win*. New Jersey: Addison-Wesley, 1971.
10. Steiner, Claude. *Scripts People Live*. New York: Grove Press, Inc., 1974.
11. Freed, Alvyn M. *TA for Kids (and Grownups Too)*. Sacramento: Jalmar Press, 1971.
12. Ernst, Ken. *Games Students Play (and What To Do About Them)*. Milbrae: Celestial Arts, 1972.
13. Ernst, Franklin. Getting-On-With, Getting-Well-Of, and Get Winners. *Transactional Analysis Journal*. 1975, 5(3), 252.
14. Weldon, George H., unpublished illustration.
15. Hawley, MacDonald. *Growing, Growing*, Minn.: Privately published, 1973, P.4.
16. Erskine, D.R.G. The Effects of a TA Class on Socially Maladjusted High School Students. *Transactional Analysis Journal*. 1975, 5(3), 252.
17. James, Muriel, & Jongeward, Dorothy. *The People Book*. New Jersey: Addison-Wesley, 1975.
18. Freed, Alvyn M. My Parent the Robot (or the Internal Dialogue.) *Transactional Analysis Journal*.
19. Rissom, A., Altorfer, O., & Wendlinger, R. *Introduce Yourself to Trilog*. Mill Valley: Privately published, 1974.
20. Reich, Wilhelm. *Discovery of the Orgone. The Function of the Orgasm*. New York: The Noonday Press, 1942.
21. Whittaker, John. OK Street Contracts. *OK Work Funbook*. Southwest Institute of Transactional Analysis, Dallas, Texas, privately published, 1974.
22. Freed, Alvyn M. Hasseltimes & Hasselgames. *Transactional Analysis Journal*. 1968, 7 (26).
23. Goulding, Robert, & Mary Goulding. Injunctions, Decisions and Redecisions. *Transactional Analysis Journal*. 6:1, Jan. 1976.
24. Master, W. H., & Johnson, Virginia, *Human Sexual Inadequacy*. London: J. A. Churchill Ltd., 1970.
25. Legislative Highlights, The California State Psychologist, Los Angeles, Feb. 1976, Vol. XI, No. 1, Pg. 18.
26. Dreiser, Theodore. *American Tragedy*. New Jersey: Signet Books, 1973.
27. Ellis, Albert. Is There a Sexual Revolution in America? Speech on Tape, California State University, Sacramento, California, 1968.
28. Allen, James R., & Barbara Ann Allen, Scripts: The Role of Permission. *Transactional Analysis Journal*. 1972, April 2:2.
29. Mart, Larry. *Group Treatment and Intimacy*. Sacramento, California. Privately published. 1974.
30. Campos, Leonard. *Breaking the Family Curse*. Manuscript, 1975.
31. Gardner, Richard A. M.D., *The Boys and Girls Book About Divorce*, Bantam Books, Inc., 1971.

* In order of appearance.